"Crystal is a courageous young woman who [...] into triumph. After witnessing the horrific [...] ...go in the Columbine library, she transformed her life from a young girl who sought the approval of her peers to a young woman who seeks to fulfill God's purpose for her life. She is an inspiration to many who have been touched by the darkness this world holds, and she encourages her readers to seek the hope that a relationship with Christ will impart."

— MISTY and BRAD BERNALL, parents of Cassie Bernall; authors of the *New York Times* best seller *She Said Yes: The Unlikely Martyrdom of Cassie Bernall*

"Crystal Woodman Miller brings a maturity beyond her years to one of the most complex questions of the Christian life — how do we respond to the devastation and loss foisted upon us by suffering and evil? What she delivers is honest, poignant, and hope-filled encouragement to find purpose in overwhelming pain. This is an important book that captures her story and the stories of others who learned the painful but reliable lesson to trust in the God of all mercy."

— DR. WESS STAFFORD, president of Compassion International

"My daughter, Rachel, died in the tragedy at Columbine High School on April 20, 1999. Crystal's life, like ours, would be forever changed that day. Her book is a powerful and honest testimony that pain can birth purpose and that triumph can emerge from tragedy."

— DARRELL SCOTT, speaker; author of *Rachel's Tears*; father of Columbine victim Rachel Scott

"Crystal is in pursuit of God's heart and all He has for her. I not only have been encouraged by her life but also am grateful that I have had the privilege to work alongside her, reaching out to high school students across the nation."

— BRYAN OLESEN, member of the Newsboys; member of Casting Pearls

"Few books have drawn me in so quickly. In this intensely personal and beautiful story, Crystal vividly recounts one of the darkest days in American history and how God redeems all that is lost. You will not be the same after reading *Marked for Life*."

— DANNY OERTLI, author/songwriter

MARKED FOR LIFE

MARKED FOR LIFE

Choosing Hope and Discovering Purpose
After Earth-Shattering Tragedy

Crystal Woodman Miller
with Ashley Wiersma

TH1NK
P.O. Box 35001
Colorado Springs, Colorado 80935

ISBN 1-57683-936-2

Cover design by Kirk DouPonce, DogEaredDesign.com
Creative Team: Nicci Hubert, Traci Mullins, Kathy Mosier, Arvid Wallen, Bob Bubnis

Some of the anecdotal illustrations in this book are true to life and are included with the permission of the persons involved. All other illustrations are composites of real situations, and any resemblance to people living or dead is coincidental.

Descriptions of events and people are offered according to the author's best recollection. Additionally, in some cases names have been changed to protect the identity of the persons involved.

Published in association with the literary agency of Alive Communications, Inc., 7680 Goddard Street, Suite 200, Colorado Springs, Colorado 80920 (www.alivecommunications.com).

Unless otherwise identified, all Scripture quotations in this publication are taken from the HOLY BIBLE: NEW INTERNATIONAL VERSION* (NIV*). Copyright © 1973, 1978, 1984 by International Bible Society. Used by permission of Zondervan Publishing House. All rights reserved. Other versions used include: the *New American Standard Bible* (NASB), © The Lockman Foundation 1960, 1962, 1963, 1968, 1971, 1972, 1973, 1975, 1977, 1995.

Miller, Crystal Woodman, 1982-
    Marked for life : choosing hope and discovering purpose after earth-shattering tragedy / Crystal Woodman Miller, with Ashley Wiersma.
        p. cm.
Includes bibliographical references.
    ISBN 1-57683-936-2
    1. Miller, Crystal Woodman, 1982- 2. Christian biography--Colorado--Littleton. 3. Columbine High School (Littleton, Colo.)--Students--Biography. I. Wiersma, Ashley. II. Title.
    BR1725.M4463A3 2006
    248.8'6--dc22
                                2005035328

Printed in the United States of America

1 2 3 4 5 6 7 8 9 10 / 10 09 08 07 06

FOR A FREE CATALOG OF
NAVPRESS BOOKS & BIBLE STUDIES,
CALL 1-800-366-7788 (USA)
OR 1-800-839-4769 (CANADA)

To the three men in my life:

My dad, Tom Woodman, who leads from before me;
My husband, Pete Miller, who leads from beside me;
And my Lord and Savior, Jesus Christ,
who leads from within me.

I will forever be grateful for the growth and transformation I have experienced because of you.

Contents

Foreword

I will never forget April 25, 1999. On that cool, cloudy day, I stood on a makeshift stage in a shopping-center parking lot in Littleton, Colorado, in front of about seventy thousand people — all of us there to mourn the overwhelming tragedy that had occurred at Columbine High School less than a week before. I had been invited by Colorado's governor, Bill Owens, to bring a short message of hope in honor of the twelve students and one teacher who were murdered by two deeply troubled teenage boys. As I looked out over the crowd of tear-stained faces, my own hope was in knowing that the Lord would be faithful to fulfill his promise "that in all things God works for the good of those who love him, who have been called according to his purpose" (Romans 8:28).

I have seen that hope confirmed again and again in the life and testimony of Crystal Woodman Miller.

I met Crystal in December 1999 when she spoke at a press event for Operation Christmas Child, an international children's project of Samaritan's Purse. From that day forward, I have seen the Lord transform Crystal from a teenage girl grappling with the emotional scars of seeing her classmates killed to a powerful and effective witness for the saving grace of Jesus Christ.

Crystal has traveled with our Samaritan's Purse teams to many countries such as Kosovo, Honduras, and Russia to deliver Christmas gifts to hurting children. Great differences in language and culture stand between Crystal and the young victims of war, poverty, and disaster to whom she ministers, yet she has a remarkable ability to tap into the pain of her own tragic experience to bridge the gaps. Because she herself has "walk[ed] through the valley of the shadow of death" (Psalm 23:4), she instinctively recognizes and responds to the needs of those who are living with physical suffering, human cruelty, and catastrophe.

Through the years, Crystal has blossomed into a fearless spokesperson for the gospel of Jesus Christ. From speaking at youth events throughout the country to providing interviews for national media outlets, she never misses an opportunity to lift up his name.

I know that as you read this book, you will be as impressed as I am by Crystal's strength, sincerity, and commitment to the Lord. I pray that her story will inspire you to present the whole of your life as a living sacrifice to Jesus Christ. Then, like Crystal, you can be sure he will provide you with everything you need to step out in faith and to work for his glory.

— FRANKLIN GRAHAM
president and CEO, Samaritan's Purse;
president and CEO, Billy Graham Evangelistic Association

Acknowledgments

Thanks first and foremost to my family. Space does not permit mentioning you all by name, but I appreciate you more than you likely know. Your footprints are present in every aspect of my life! You've remained right by my side both through the struggles and the triumphs — we have cried together, laughed together, and celebrated life together. But most important, you have shown me the limitless love of Jesus Christ. Thank you for continually inspiring me to live for his glory.

An extra special thanks to Pete, my faithful husband and best friend. You truly are my rock, and you have shown me nothing but love and support every step of the way. You provide me with all the necessary inspiration to pursue my every dream! God has given me the most precious gift I could ask for in you.

Thanks to my family at Bridgeway Church and Jezreel Community. You have taught me what it truly means to be a passionate seeker of Christ and have shown me how a community in love with Jesus operates. You are the ones I love to do life with day after day. Perhaps God brought Pete and me to Oklahoma simply to experience the power of his Spirit working through you, our brothers and sisters in Christ. Thank you for allowing God to speak through your worship, preaching, and teaching, and most of all through your love for one another and for me.

Thanks to my "Colorado pastor," Gino Geraci. You never stopped believing in me and challenging me to grow.

This book would never have been what it is without the help of my writer, Ashley Wiersma, a dear friend and partner who has poured herself into this project, heart and soul. Because of the countless hours we have spent together and the dozens of journals you have read, you now know me better than most. And still you show me deep, abiding love. I not only respect your gifts as a writer but also value your opinions on life — I feel like I could talk to you about anything! Thank you for all of your time and attention.

I am who I am today because of the way God has used the people and experiences at Samaritan's Purse and Operation Christmas Child. You have provided endless opportunities to pursue my passion for international ministry and have allowed me to develop skills that have shaped me for the future. Thank you for your commitment to the call of Christ to serve those who are hurting around the world. Thanks also to my friends I've lived with overseas for so many poignant memories and life-altering experiences.

Thank you to my editor, Traci Mullins, who with wisdom, expertise, and sharp skills chiseled away the original manuscript until a work of art could emerge. What a wonderful privilege it has been to partner with you on this project! Thanks also to the entire TH1NK team at NavPress Publishing. You gave me the gift of an avenue through which to steward the story God has given me! And you did a fantastic job coming up with a title for that story — a title that really does epitomize my journey so far. I am honored to be working with such a reputable organization and such caring individuals.

A true God-ordained moment happened the day I met my literary agent, Beth Jusino of Alive Communications. When it seemed no one else could grasp the vision of this project, you showed up with passion and energy for it. As a result, I have the opportunity to see the fulfillment of a years-old dream. Thank you for never giving up and for allowing me to share my heart.

Where would any of us be without friends? I have some of the most patient and loving friends imaginable. Some of you have walked with me since childhood throughout this journey called life. Others I've known only for a few months, but you have already been an unmatched source of strength, love, and encouragement. Thank you for talking some sense into me when I wanted to throw in the towel along the way. You all are cherished people who have been incredibly instrumental to my learning more of what it means to be a true friend and devoted follower of Christ. I love you!

And finally, my heart bursts with gratitude for the love and salvation-gift of Jesus Christ, through whom all things have been given and made possible. There is *nothing* more I want than for his heart to beat in mine, his blood to flow through my veins, and his breath to fill me up and enable me to share his message of hope with the world! May this book be received as an act of worship. I believe it was written through the empowerment of the Holy Spirit, and I trust that it will support his work in the hearts and lives of its readership. It is an unspeakable joy to be counted a child of his, and I am humbled by the opportunity he has given me to participate in the creation of this book. May all I do be to his glory now and always.

Giving It All Away

"What I have said, that will I bring about;
what I have planned, that will I do."
ISAIAH 46:11

Our Russian ministry guide, Sergey, silently led us to the deserted classroom where many of the lives had been taken. I stepped carefully over the huge holes onto slices of floor that remained, noticing papers with children's handwriting on them, pictures drawn by young hands, dolls, flowers intended for teachers, books, clothes, and shoes littering every inch of the wide classrooms. Bricks and wood pieces and chunks of cement were strewn about, and the blood spatterings that covered bullet-hole-riddled walls overwhelmed my senses.

We reached the classroom, and Sergey stood off to the side of our small group. "You may notice the ceiling, the walls," Sergey began.

As he continued, I looked up and spotted what seemed to be millions of burnt orange flecks dotting the gray walls and ceiling.

"What you see there are actually bits and pieces of them — bits and pieces of the too-young victims and the terrorists who blew themselves up after committing this heinous act against our community and against our country."

I covered my mouth with one hand and held my stomach with the other as it flipped over inside of me. *What kind of evil person would do this to innocent people — to children even?* I wondered.

I'd been in Beslan only a day, but for weeks my mind had been swimming in the details of the school hostage situation that had rocked this small town just three months earlier. I had joined a ministry team that was there to provide tangible encouragement to the families and friends of the victims — and to many of the survivors who had miraculously made it out alive. During the six years that had passed since the devastation at my alma mater, Columbine High School, I had experienced my fair share of ups and downs, but I had learned that the only thing that could dispel the darkness I had faced was the illuminating light of Christ. I was absolutely compelled to go share this hope with a community so badly in need of it. Through Operation Christmas Child, a ministry for which I had become one of several national spokespeople, I hoped I could bring some light into the darkness of southwestern Russia.

Hell on Earth

On September 1, 2004, a warm and otherwise beautiful morning in the North Ossetia town of Beslan, Russia, two unmarked vans pulled up to the front of Beslan School No. 1. Thirty-two heavily armed men and women suddenly formed two lines and streamed across the front and side perimeters of the building. Soon enough, they would be identified as Islamic fundamentalist terrorists and would be known for their devastating legacy of taking more than twelve hundred men, women, and children hostage, a fourth of whom would never make it out alive, according to published reports. It was around 9:20 in the morning, and mothers and fathers were still escorting their children into the school for what Russians call The Day of Knowledge.

During the summer months, Russian children and teachers anxiously prepare for the first day of school much like Americans do for a graduation ceremony. When that magical day finally arrives, entire families head to school with their children — kids who joyfully approach the building with balloons and small gifts in hand for their teachers. For first graders entering the school that initial time, The Day of Knowledge is an unparalleled celebration. Teachers go to incredible lengths to make sure everything about that day is perfect for those six- and seven-year-olds, recognizing that it is a day those little ones will likely remember for the rest of their lives.

How true that would be this particular year.

The terrorists popped the air above the crowd with hundreds of rounds of gunfire as they shoved parents, teachers, and students into the small gymnasium. The school served first graders through eleventh graders, and older students who had the presence of mind to escape did so immediately. But the vast majority of those who had gathered for the first day of school that morning were caught so off guard they could do nothing but protect their heads from raining bullets and race into the gym at the terrorists' demand.

The conditions inside were horrendous. The sun was high in the sky by then, and the already-hot room seemed to grow more and more stifling by the hour. Later reports would say that bodies were piled into the gym like herring in a barrel. Video images that came out after the attack confirmed just how accurate that description was.

Eventually, terrorists removed the last of the hostages' privileges — water and access to bathroom facilities. Mothers and fathers and children were forced to relieve themselves in public. Then, to fend off imminent dehydration, they resorted to drinking their own urine.

Bombs had been rigged to the basketball hoops and attached to a detonating device that was on the floor. A terrorist had his foot positioned firmly on the pedal for what would be a three-day standoff;

hostages were well aware that if he released his foot even for a second, the bombs would instantly explode.

In the early afternoon hours of September 3, a bomb dangling from the basketball hoop unexpectedly blew up, possibly the result of the hostage taker's fatigue or disorientation after not having slept in more than fifty hours. Immediately, all hell broke loose. Russian special forces who had surrounded the building stormed the two-story facility, picking off one terrorist at a time. Snatching up children and using them as human shields, the hostage takers fought back in a warlike battle that lasted for nearly ten hours. In the end, 330 people were confirmed dead, 176 of them young children. Between five hundred and seven hundred others were wounded — some severely so — and twenty-four children were left to grow up as orphans.[1] (Having seen firsthand the school and the row upon row of tombstones, I'd venture to guess that the numbers were actually much higher.)

"Let Them Know I Know . . ."

Interestingly, Beslan was so much like my own hometown of Littleton — like any small town in America, for that matter. With just over thirty thousand residents, the little Russian community enjoyed tight bonds and strong values. Kids rode their bikes on warm days, enjoyed video games, and frequently dreamed about what they'd be when they grew up.

In the weeks leading up to my trip, I talked candidly with God, telling him how desperately I wanted the children from Beslan to see me as one of them rather than some American snob who couldn't relate to tragedy on that level. More than that, I wanted them to see Christ in me — to see care and concern, despite the fact that we didn't know each other and couldn't even speak the same language. I wanted them to know that I loved them and that there was a God who loved them and would never leave them.

While in Moscow the day before our team was to visit Beslan, I conveyed my desires to God — the only steady force in my roller-coaster experience of a life:

> *God, I ask for your Spirit to lead and guide us every step of the way. You've already done so much in getting us through customs and seeing to the details of our travel plans. I believe you brought us here for a very special purpose, and I really want to be used, to be poured out, for your glory. I want to have an impact here, God! I ask you for divine encounters with many of the kids I'll meet while I'm in Russia. Please use my story to touch the lives of those children. I know beyond the shadow of a doubt that I went through Columbine so that I might love and help others. I pray that I would be able to connect supernaturally with the children and families and friends of the victims there — let them know that I know. I know of the pain. The confusion. The grief. The hopelessness. But I also know that things can get better.*
>
> *Use my words, use my expressions, use my actions, use my open arms to bring healing to these precious people. As we distribute shoeboxes that contain gifts and the gospel presentation, please soften the hearts of the Russian government officials so that they will enable the encouragement to reach their people. I pray for an absolute miracle there! Please fill me up in every regard, so I can give, give, give it all away. Here I am, Lord. Use me however you please in Russia. I love you!*

Give it all away. It had become the earnest desire of my heart. To take what I had been given in the days since I thought my life was over — peace, contentedness, encouragement, purpose, hope — and to just give it all away.

So much had changed in the lifetime I'd lived since Columbine.

When our team first arrived, Sergey led us directly into the gymnasium, where the majority of the Beslan tragedy unfolded. I had begged God to prepare me for what I was about to see, but nothing could prepare a person for such horror. As I climbed out of the car, I couldn't bring myself to look at the building because I knew the minute I did, I'd absolutely lose it.

Sure enough, as I turned around and began walking up to the school, the sorrow welled up and poured out of me in heaves while I stared at a building that had entire sections missing — signs of an all-out war. I had been to war-torn countries before and seen the effects, but this was different — *this* war had been waged against innocent, unarmed children.

My heart ached.

I had brought with me several roses that I'd intended to place at the school as a sign of love and respect, but once I arrived, the gesture just didn't seem like enough. I stood there sobbing, imagining the horror that had taken place.

The halls were lit only by hazy sunbeams that struggled to permeate the soiled windows. As we crossed the threshold to enter the gym, our hearts and minds were instantly sobered. Without words, our attitudes and postures reflected our deep, heartfelt reverence for the lives so senselessly lost there.

Sergey didn't have to give one word of explanation regarding the significance of where we stood; the news stories and briefs our team had received prior to the trip gave point-by-point details of all that had occurred in that room.

I stood in place, craning my head to the right and to the left, taking in the scene as it appeared now. Three months later, the gym still bore signs of murder and destruction. I imagined the terrorists with their faces masked, screaming out threats at the children, their hands holding guns, their feet on the bombs. I imagined them with hatred in their eyes, mowing down anyone who stood in their path. I imagined the overwhelming evil that had surrounded that place.

But I also saw God, his legion of angels fighting valiantly for each person inside. Reports reveal that kids inside were, in fact, praying with one another, and many may even have come to know Jesus personally in those final moments.

The gym showed signs of the fresh layer of snow that had recently fallen, its drifts undeterred because the roof above had been blown off. Most of the sentiments and memorials from visitors were now covered by white, puffy flakes — a sign, I hoped, that all things would be made fresh and new somehow.

My gaze was drawn to an old balance beam in the hallway that was adjacent to the gym, now coated with dust and debris and pock-marked like a hail-damaged car hood. I took several steps toward the beam, stopping when I noticed what was perched on top of it: a boy's small black dress shoe. Tears flooded my eyes as I considered the implications of all those young boys and girls suffering through such torment. I felt my heart break inside my chest with what seemed like a burden for our world at large.

As a sixteen-year-old who faced seven minutes of unthinkable shock and horror in a high school library, I had experienced terror unlike anything I'd ever known. But I wondered what it must have been like for kids much younger than I had been to suffer through such unimaginable fear and anguish and pain for three days straight. Reports later confirmed that the terrorists had allowed eleven mothers with their infants to exit the school safely during the siege, but each one was leaving an older school-aged child inside.[2] Can you imagine having to make that decision — choosing between staying in a deplorable situation where guns are pointed at your head while your infant wails from lack of clean air, water, and food; and hugging your older child good-bye, possibly for the last time ever, as you seek protection for your baby? It is incomprehensible.

For Such a Time As This

As we made our way out of the school and back into our van, we passed once more the makeshift memorial that townspeople had created in honor of the hundreds of lives lost. There were flowers and notes and signs all over the place. But most poignantly, there were hundreds of full bottles of water lining the gym floor — a moving reflection of the community's deep desire to quench the thirst of those who had suffered.

As hard as I tried to stay present with the current situation, I found myself taken back in my mind's eye to Clement Park near Columbine High School in those first days following April 20, 1999. I saw the tall mounds of thoughtful letters and flowers and posters with pictures of my deceased classmates. I saw hundreds of stuffed animals, poems, peace ribbons, banners. I saw big wooden crosses that had been erected for each person killed. I saw disillusioned parents and teachers and coaches and friends walking like zombies through the field of remembrance.

And then I multiplied it by a factor of more than *twenty*. I felt so unworthy to be in Beslan, Russia, trying to offer hope and encouragement to survivors and their families. But something deep inside told me that I had endured Columbine for such a time as this.

This community of Beslan had lost so much in such a short time. Now they were being asked to do the impossible: to make progress inch by inch toward the tomorrows of their lives. But despite their heartfelt efforts, I knew there was a question haunting each and every one of them: Would real healing ever come?

Our next stop would prove to be an unbelievably challenging experience. Sergey led us to the cemetery where hundreds of gravestones — mostly small, simple heaps of dirt — had been added in the ninety days since September 1.

We walked slowly along the rows of wreaths and flowers, candy and teddy bears, and water bottles, respectful of the family members gathered that day to openly weep at the loss of their young sons or daughters, mothers or fathers. As was tradition in most of Russia, tombs were marked with photographs of the deceased, and the tiny features staring back at me were painful reminders of the awfulness of it all.

I came upon several graves for the Tatiev children. Having read dozens of articles and interviews regarding the Tatiev family, our team was all too familiar with the tragic story. Bella Tatiev had lost four of her five young children at Beslan School No. 1. Bella's husband was a pastor in Russia, as was his brother. The brother and his wife, Rosen, had lost two of their children in that massacre as well — six of eight cousins senselessly killed in a three-day period.

I stood at the Tatiev plot containing six small mounds of dirt and heard the rest of my team approach from behind. There were no words to describe the sorrow we all felt, so we stood there for several minutes in perfect silence as the snow began to fall.

Slowly but Surely

I rejoined the rest of my team as they were entering Beslan School No. 6, the site of our next shoebox distribution. While the catalyst for our trip to Russia was our desire to serve the families and friends of siege victims, we took advantage of the unprecedented access our team was given to spread hope to the neighboring schools and communities that were reeling from the horrific events as well.

It was an eerie feeling as we walked upstairs and entered the gymnasium of the school that was up and running as if tragedy had never touched a neighboring school. At once it hit us all that the room we were standing in must have looked identical to the gym at School No. 1 before the siege took place. The basketball hoops in this gymnasium were perfectly hung with nothing dangling beneath them. The ceiling was pristine, the walls unmarred. The equipment was all in its place, ready for use by animated and energetic young boys and girls eager for a break from classroom work. The crowd gathered there to hear our team's presentations that day numbered about three hundred. I took note of how full the room seemed, trying to imagine how in the world twelve hundred men, women, and children had been stuffed into a room the same size just a few months earlier.

A children's choir sang several songs before our team's director, Hans, was introduced. He conveyed our desire that the hundreds of shoeboxes we were about to put into their hands would provide light in a dark situation. He reminded the audience that God is bigger than our circumstances, that he cares for the needs of his people, and that he loves us all with an everlasting love.

The energy and excitement in the room was pulsating as we began the distribution. Children raced to open their boxes, overjoyed when they found hats and balls and coloring books inside. As the minutes ticked by, I discerned a shift in the countenance of even the toughest hearts present. A Russian special forces officer who had been eyeing our team with sternness during the entire presentation finally joined us in passing out shoeboxes. She smiled for the first time that day as she saw delight creep across the faces of previously skittish children. Miraculously, she even began passing out Russian booklets we had brought; the title in English read *The Greatest Gift of All*. Whether knowingly or not, she was sharing the gospel message with hundreds of children as she placed the pamphlets in those little palms!

As my team prepared to depart from School No. 6, a realization struck me with powerful force: *That was me! I too was a kid without hope, without a life, without a future. But by the grace of God, look at me now!* And in a flood of emotion, I felt God wrap his loving arms around me and remind me that although I *had been* that kid, I didn't have to be hopeless forever. When Columbine happened, I thought everything was over. But God made it clear I was marked for life, not marked for death. Marked for a purpose, not marked for useless-ness. Marked for hope, not marked for senseless suffering.

In those moments I could feel myself releasing more of the anguish and fear and despair I'd so faithfully clung to. I realized that I really could discard the anger and resentment and bitterness. I could turn my back on the misery that had become part of the fabric of my young life, choosing instead to hand God the broken pieces and witness a miracle as he masterfully put them back together again. Despite all of the realities that would still exist in my crazy personality, hopelessness didn't have to be one of them. Never, ever again.

A Heart Now Grateful

Our team sat in the muggy airport awaiting our final flight home. Once on board, I reached into my bag to grab a bottle of water, thanking God with renewed gratitude for the life I was now living. I wasn't being held against my will, and therefore I was free. I wasn't denied food or water or basic needs of life, and therefore I was rich. I wasn't without hope, and therefore I was truly alive!

As I stuffed the bottle back into my pack, I noticed a small plastic yo-yo sitting at the bottom, its stark white string begging to be spun. It was red all over, both sides bearing a brightly painted smiley face. A little boy had placed it in the palm of my hand in Beslan, earnestly gesturing that he wanted me to keep it.

I grinned as I pictured his wispy brown hair, chubby young fingers, big brown eyes — so full of unsuppressed optimism and evident joy despite his understandable sadness. He had been given more than the gift of time and more than the gift of gifts. Through our efforts there, I like to believe that he had been given a chance to be a kid again, if even for a moment.

The memory of the day he handed me his brand-new yo-yo will stick with me forever. Despite all that he had been through, and in the midst of having so little, somehow he was still determined to give, give, give it all away.

Exactly as I'm going to do for the rest of my days, I thought as I flipped it over in my hand and smiled at the smiley face grinning back at me. *Give, give, give it all away.*

CHAPTER ONE

Columbines Everywhere

Our hope is that nothing can separate us from the love of God in Christ, not even suffering and death. Our hope is not for an easy or comfortable or secure life on this earth. Our hope is that the love of God will grant us joy in the all-satisfying glory of God which will continue through death and increase for all eternity.

JOHN PIPER, "A SERVICE OF SORROW, SELF-HUMBLING, AND STEADY HOPE IN OUR SAVIOR AND KING, JESUS CHRIST: A RESPONSE TO THE ATTACK ON THE WORLD TRADE CENTER"

I'm a huge fan of the *Today* show. In fact, hardly a day goes by that I don't catch at least part of it. It's uplifting and informative. And somehow, my day is just a little more complete when it's kicked off with Katie, Matt, and Al.

One morning in 2005, though, the snippets of headlines that reached my ears while I was boiling water for my wild orange hot tea felt like an assault. *Officer tells of finding eight-year-old Florida girl buried alive. Bomb kills at least ten at Baghdad restaurant. Supreme Court reenters abortion debate. Blasts rock two New Delhi cinemas. Pastor arrested in child sex ring.*

Wasn't there any good news out there? It reminded me of the days after Columbine when my family and friends and I sat glued to the TV, absorbing more information, more bad news, about all that had gone on the morning of April 20, 1999.

This morning, unable to brush the memory aside, I turned off the TV, walked into the study, and went online to do a search on school-related shootings in the last few years. I knew other ones had occurred, and for some reason I just needed to know that day that someone else out there could relate to what I was going through. I was shocked by what appeared on the screen.

A pale blue chart popped up, detailing line-by-line accounts of school shootings in various places around the world. This particular list dated back to 1996 when a fourteen-year-old boy opened fire on his algebra class, killing two students and a teacher and wounding another student. *How long* is *this list?* I thought as I scrolled fever-ishly to the next screen, and the next, and the next.

I counted forty incidents. Nearly five hundred innocent people dead.

As I scrolled back to the top of the gruesome inventory, my eyes darted up and down, taking in a random assortment of the descriptions:

- March 1997: Mohammad Ahman al-Naziri killed eight people in two different schools in Sanaa, Yemen.
- April 26, 2002: A nineteen-year-old student at Johann Gutenberg secondary school in Erfurt, Germany, killed thir-teen teachers, two students, and one policeman and wounded ten others before killing himself.
- February 29, 2000: Six-year-old Kayla Rolland was shot dead in her elementary school by a six-year-old boy in her class (yes, six years old!) who had possession of a .32-caliber handgun.
- September 1, 2004: The Beslan school siege.

- February 19, 1997: A sixteen-year-old boy in Bethel, Alaska, shot and killed his principal and a fellow student.
- March 21, 2005: Sixteen-year-old Jeff Weise killed his grandfather and companion before arriving at school in Red Lake, Minnesota, where he killed a teacher, a security guard, five students, and finally himself.[1]
- May 21, 1998: A fifteen-year-old student in Springfield, Oregon, who had been arrested a day earlier for bringing a gun to school, killed two students and wounded twenty-two others after shooting and killing both parents at home earlier that day.
- December 1997: Michael Carneal, age fourteen, shot and killed three students and wounded two others, all of whom were participating in a prayer circle at Heath High School in West Paducah, Kentucky.

I did a double take when I saw Columbine listed among so many other similar events. The tragedy that had stolen my friends' lives and forever changed the worlds of thousands of people in Colorado was just one of nearly three dozen others. The plain description noted only the facts:

> April 20, 1999, Littleton, Colo.: 14 students (including killers) and one teacher killed, 23 others wounded at Columbine High School in the nation's deadliest school shooting. Eric Harris, 18, and Dylan Klebold, 17, had plotted for a year to kill at least 500 and blow up their school. At the end of their hour-long rampage, they turned their guns on themselves.[2]

I thought I'd moved on from the horrors of Columbine — and I suppose in many ways I had. But as I stared at my computer screen, reading and rereading that sterile paragraph, the memories marched through my mind, my heart, my throat. It was all happening again, in real time.

Darkest of Days

The Colorado skies are hazy and gray that early spring morning. The sound of my father's heavy-duty pickup truck pulling out of our driveway interrupts what has been a deep sleep. I twitch my cheek and wonder where my good-morning kiss is as I try to remember why he's leaving so early today. *It's his busy season*, I decide. *Maybe he has a meeting before his landscaping appointments.* I stuff my pillow farther under my chin, propping my head up so I can make out the numbers on the clock. 6:32, it proudly beams. *Ugh, seventeen minutes late already, and I'm still not out of bed.*

I flop onto my back, now suddenly enamored by the way the shadows are hitting the ceiling above me. *I gotta get going*, I think. "Okay, get going," I say, groaning. Groggily padding into the bathroom, I stick a toothbrush in my mouth to kick off the daily routine. I step into the hot shower and am jolted awake by a strong sense that today will not be an ordinary day. *What is it?* I wonder as I point my face toward the shower head. *It's my dad*, I realize as my heart sinks. *Something bad is going to happen to him today, I just know it. A car accident?* My mind trails off as I try to decode the eerie premonition. I can't shake the anxious feelings but know I have to get moving if I will stand half a chance of being on time for first period.

Clothes. I need clothes. I hop unsteadily into my favorite jeans, thrusting my feet into a pair of cute sandals as I pull on a green-and-navy-striped sweater tank and a navy fleece jacket. I comb my wet shoulder-length blondish brown hair and hastily brush on mascara as I hustle around my room shoving stuff into my backpack. *I'm so scattered today. Maybe I'm still coming down off prom,*

I think in my own defense. I eye my French-manicured nails, leftovers from the dance just a few nights ago. *They still look so good!* I relish the memory of feeling like a princess in my stark white tealength gown.

Mom interrupts my thoughts of James and friends and laughter and dancing as she cranes her head around my open bedroom door. "Gotta run, sweetie," she says as she blows me a kiss.

I'm in too big of a rush to ask why she's dressed up so early in the morning, so I opt instead for a quick response. "Bye, Mom. I love you!" I holler, meaning it.

Wheeling around to make sure I haven't forgotten anything, I glance at my beloved alarm clock once more. 7:24, the numbers glare. No breakfast today — again. "Four hours till lunch," I mutter to myself. "I can make it."

At the first stoplight en route to school, my morning turns from bad to worse as I remember I'm supposed to take a make-up physics exam this afternoon. *When am I going to study for this stupid test? It's today! How could I have forgotten that?* The light turns to green as I land on a plan. *Lunch! I'll make Seth and Sara ask me review questions all period. I'll be fine. We'll hit the library instead of going off-campus to eat, and they'll make sure I'm ready.* I crank up the radio again and head toward Columbine.

It's 7:35 as I pull into my assigned parking spot in the parking lot designated for juniors, a little late but probably not enough to land me in trouble. My toes freeze as I step out of my car into what is now a cool drizzle and head for the entrance. *April in the Rockies*, I remember. *You never know what you're going to get.* I wrap my fleece jacket tighter around me, wishing I had made a wiser shoe selection.

First period is drudgery but finally ends. I walk into second period — math class — and ease into my desk, finally waking up after a good night's rest cut short. My friends and I stop chatting as the monitor in the corner buzzes to life with today's video announcements. Today's anchors are a couple of kids from media class who were selected to host the broadcast on our school's Rebel News Network.

Seeing nothing that intrigues us about today's news, my girlfriends and I giggle back to life only half-listening to today's lunch menu, the location of the baseball team's next game, and when yearbooks will be available. As usual, the broadcast ends with a ticker-tape quote across the bottom of the screen that today is running to really bad techno pop. I look up as it crawls across the monitor:

> **... April ... 20 ... 1999 ... You'll ... wish ... you ... weren't ... here ... today ...**

Well, what's new? I think to myself. *I wish that every day! I mean, I live by the mountains. Who does want to be at school? I could be home sleeping or hiking or biking in the Rockies — anything would be better than this. How stupid.*

❧

Two periods later, I sit through Mr. Webb's language arts class and grow more anxious by the minute. *The lunch bell's about to ring, and then I can bolt,* I think in an effort to calm myself down. My physics test is looming, and I know I will have to pull off a bona fide cramming extravaganza in order to pass.

The shrill *Brrrrrrrrring* bursts through Mr. Webb's homework instructions, and I grab my backpack, stuffing my language arts textbook into the largest pocket as I fly toward the door. Instantly, I am greeted by my friend Seth who, unbeknownst to him, is one-third of my study team for our working lunch. I grab his arm and head toward the library — surely a better bet than the cafeteria for some quiet study time — as I explain that he's going to have to help me instead of enjoying a nice, normal lunch.

"Seth, I forgot to study last night, and my physics make-up test is this afternoon. You have to quiz me over lunch! Please?" I beg. As we swim upstream through the flood of students racing to and from McDonald's or Taco Bell in fifty minutes or less, me groveling with each step, we both head toward the lockers to find Seth's sister Sara. She says she is starving and wants to know where we're eating today. Seth raises his eyebrows with a grin and cuts his eyes toward me as if to say, *Ask Crystal. She has her own plans for us today.* He doesn't seem to care what we do — he grabbed a bagel during his off-period just moments before.

Sara groans but decides to join us anyway. We can't bring cafeteria trays or fast food into the library, so Sara and I will just starve. Now I really wish I had eaten breakfast.

⚜

The library is strangely empty as we walk in and head toward several tables in the center section. *Must have warmed up enough to eat outside*, I think to myself. Seth lags behind and looks perplexed when I cross without incident through the security detectors positioned on either side of the library's entrance. They were installed a few years prior as a way to keep kids from thieving books, magazines, videos, or CDs instead of checking them out.

"Let's sit there," I say as I nod toward an empty table. As I pull my chair out from the heavy oak table, my eyes catch the rays of sun now flooding through the library's floor-to-ceiling west windows. *Sure, now that I'm stuck in here studying, the sun comes out!*

The three of us get settled and take a look around the library. "There's really *nobody* here," Sara says as we all eye the empty computer workstations, vacant study tables, and deserted reception desk. I let my backpack thud to the ground beside my chair and lean down to pull out my physics book. As I yank it out, a dorky science magazine falls to the floor. "What's this?" I ask Seth and Sara.

"Well, let's just say you're detector-proof," Seth says with a wry smile. "I stuck it in your stuff last Friday to get you busted next time we came in here, but it didn't go off!" I slowly roll up the magazine with a grin, ready to whack him upside the head as he tries to get himself out of the doghouse. Our mock argument catches the librarian's attention, and she is none too pleased. *Where'd she come from, anyway?* We nod our acceptance of her *Pipe down!* gaze and determine to get to work.

Still in denial that it's time to help me study, Seth hops up dutifully to return the stolen magazine to its appropriate shelf near the computer workstations. Sara stares at me as I thumb through the physics chapters I have to memorize in forty minutes' time. "Thirty-six pages!" I yelp as she giggles. "There's no way!"

I sigh as I swear for the nth time to stay on top of my schoolwork.

While I'm in midthought, a teacher I don't know bursts into the library. She looks crazed and utterly panicked. I hadn't noticed the several dozen or so students who had filled the tables around us until I look to their faces to make sense of the interruption.

"There are guys with guns!" the teacher screams. She is frantic, rushing back and forth across the east side of the library. "They've got bombs! Do you hear me? Bombs and guns! They are shooting at students! Move . . . now! Get under your tables *now*," she belts. Her voice is cracking, her hands flailing around her face that still looks white as a sheet.

There is palpable tension in the air as all of us stare at this hysterical woman. *Is this a joke? A senior prank?* I wonder. I look at Seth, a senior himself, to see if he's in on the hoax. *Graduation is a month away*, I reason. *The video class is up to something — it's just some weird project.*

I stay in my chair, waiting for everyone else to make a move that will tell me this isn't for real. In the halls outside the library, I hear students running and screaming, but it all sounds so distant, so bizarre.

"Where's Mrs. Keating? Mrs. Keating!" the distraught teacher shouts. The librarian doesn't respond. *Strange*, I think. *Mrs. Keating was just at the reception desk a few minutes ago. Where'd she go?*

The woman jerks her head toward Sara and me and demands again that we get under our tables. Seth runs over to the windows to see what is happening, then reemerges and looks at me with calm eyes. "It's just the lunch rush," he says. "Everything's fine." Without fully buying his explanation, I covet his steadiness.

The panicked teacher hasn't settled down yet, and her hysteria is making everyone's heart pound out dull, heavy beats. I look behind her at a student who is stumbling into the library, his right hand clutching his left shoulder. Blood is soaking through his T-shirt. He falls to the floor just in front of the security detectors, and the room fills with gasps and shrieks of horror.

I feel my chest rise and my chin drop as I try to stabilize myself. "My God, he's bleeding! What do we do? What do we do?" I sputter in Seth's direction. My peripheral vision catches the bleeding student stagger toward the break room behind the reception desk. "Seth, what's going on?" I plead. "I mean it, what's going on? What is *happening*, Seth?"

Nothing but silence from my friend.

I hear more running, more screaming coming from the halls as another person rushes through the entrance. A man I recognize as Mr. Long, the technical education teacher, is desperately sputtering out commands, insisting that everyone leave the library immediately. "Get out of here now!" he shouts in our direction.

The first teacher yells at us again, her quaking voice breaking as she gets louder with each phrase. "Everyone stay under your desks! Students! Heads on the floor and do . . . not . . . MOVE!"

Each student's face registers confusion and panic. *Who do we listen to? Which direction do we go? What are we supposed to do, get under our tables or run out of here?*

Mr. Long is gone as quickly as he arrived, and as he bolts back through the library's entrance to reenter the school's hallway, I hear escalating shrieks and pops and shouting.

"Everyone stay under your desks!" the lady shouts a final time with authority, as if to settle our confusion once and for all. I hear her rush to the reception counter, where she picks up the receiver and dials the three numbers that prove this is definitely not a senior prank: 911.

"Yes. I am a teacher at Columbine High School," she starts, her composure strangely regained as she shifts into calm-and-collected mode. "There is a student here with a gun. He has shot out a window . . . I believe . . . um . . . STUDENTS, DOWN!" she interrupts herself with previous hysteria as popping sounds flood our ears. "UNDER THE TABLES, KIDS! HEADS UNDER THE TABLES!"

Something is wrong! What's going on? I think as Seth, Sara, and I fumble over each other to crawl underneath the table. Our arms and legs are flailing about as the three of us stuff our bodies uneasily under a four-foot-tall wooden table. I land just in front of Seth, my head in his lap, my eyes fixed on his knees and shoes, my back to the library entrance.

I direct my eyes toward his as he says, "There's nothing to worry about, Crys — " But before he gets to the second syllable of my name, an explosion goes off in the hallway. "Crystal," he says as if to complete his thought, "those are paintball guns and firecrackers. There's nothing to worry about, I promise."

With all of my heart, I want to believe Seth. He's one of my closest friends — he'd never let *anything* happen to me. And plus, nothing bad ever happens in Littleton, Colorado! This is our town — our secure, intact bubble of alrightness. There are no gang problems here. There's no huge drug ring in operation. I quickly focus on the other school shootings I'd heard about in recent months, deciding that Littleton is no West Paducah. It's *safe* here!

As the popping sounds and shrieks get louder and closer, Seth defies his own reassurances and lies down beside me, wrapping his arms tightly around my head. Sara, who had been sitting near my feet, now huddles close to me, hanging on to my waist and legs. She's nearly my own age — only one grade behind me — but over the years she has become like a little sister to me.

Sara and I are shaking and whimpering as the strange sounds get louder and louder. "What's happening?" I beg Seth as tears pop into my eyes. I am scared to make any sound, and so I hold back my need to cry.

Seth's strength shifts into high gear as he tries to convince me that everything is okay. "Crystal, don't worry. But listen, we need to start praying. Sara, you too. Whatever is going on, God is the only one who can get us through this. Pray, Crystal."

My heart skips a beat as the fire alarm suddenly blares. I hadn't realized how much smoke had flooded into the library from the explosion until now. My mind shudders. *I didn't know things could get any louder!*

"Calm down, Crystal, calm down," Seth urges as he cups my head in his hands. "Start praying. Please just start praying now."

Breathing requires special effort as my mind frantically tries to make sense of the sights and sounds and smells surrounding me. Above the popping and shrieking and blaring fire alarms, I can hear my own heartbeat pounding in my chest.

God, please protect us. Please send the police to get us out of here. Please, God, please send your angels to help us. I pray in short, unspoken bursts, each silent plea more intense and intentional than the one before.

The hallway sounds are so close that I find myself burying my head deeper and deeper into Seth's chest. *Which direction are they coming from? From the right or from the left?* Somehow it doesn't matter. The truth is they are heading straight for the library. And they are rapidly getting closer.

"Crystal," Seth begins, his tone serious, his cadence slow, "I want you to know that I will take a bullet for you. I promise you that I'll take a bullet for you."

I feel myself begin to hyperventilate. *What is he talking about, taking a bullet for me? Is someone going to be shooting at me?* A wave of denial washes over me as I refuse to believe that I really am in danger, that my life really is at stake. *My God! I'm a junior in high school! Why is he talking like this?*

As I contemplate my own death for the very first time, I see images of family and friends rush across my mind's eye. I am gripped by instant replays of the stupid decisions I've made, the ridiculous things I've done in my past. I start to wonder what it will be like — what it will *feel* like — to be shot. *Will it hurt? Will I know it once I've been shot? Will it paralyze me? What if I can't play sports or walk again? Or what if it just kills me altogether? Will it be instant death, or will I have to suffer and gasp and writhe in pain?*

I scoot in closer to Seth, believing his presence will eradicate the overwhelming nausea that is now rising into my throat. *Voices. I hear new voices.* Two evil voices are booming through the library now, filled with spite and anger and rage, as the popping noises come closer.

"We've been waiting our whole lives for this day!" one of them sneers. "This is for all of you who picked on us and made fun of us!"

"Yeah! This is for all of you!" announces the other.

I instantly realize that these voices are from the "guys with guns" that the frenzied teacher warned the 911 operator about moments ago, but their words are spewed with such evil, such hatred, that to me they sound like grown men. I can't see their faces, their bodies, their weapons, but suddenly, gunfire sprays the library walls and several bombs explode. I choke back a cough from the smoke, hesitant to make a sound.

"Everyone stand up!" one of them hollers. "Get out from underneath your tables," he shouts as he sprays gunfire across the floor.

Nobody moves.

"All the jocks — get up!" he screams, his voice straining to rise above the incessant fire alarms and distracting strobe lights that shine blinding rounds of light across the room. Still, no movement.

"Jocks, you're all dead," the voice says. "If you have a white T-shirt or a white hat, say your good-byes. You're dead."

I hear a voice from across the room. "Why are you doing this to us?" a girl shouts out.

He responds to her question with gunfire, shaking the entire room with explosions. *This is what hell must be like,* I think as I try to control my shaking body. *The trembling won't stop. . . . I can't get it to stop.*

I hear an exchange between the gunmen and Isaiah, a senior who is a football player at Columbine. He is crouched under a table in the section next to ours, and they are taunting him, naming him with pejorative terms. I desperately want the racial slurs and abuse to stop, but I know there is nothing I can do from where I lie.

Several shots are fired, followed by an evil voice. "Is he dead?" he asks. "Yeah. He's dead," the other replies. *Isaiah?* I wonder. *They just killed Isaiah?*

I shudder as I listen to the satisfaction in their voices as they shoot one student after another. Each murder is a victory in their estimation — cause for loud whooping and celebration. *I'm next,* I tell myself. *I know I'm next.* With each round of gunfire, the floor shakes and reverberates, threatening to cave in on the cafeteria below. I find myself concentrating on breathing through the smoke, desperately taking in puffs of air as if they must be rationed. My flesh grows numb in spots where shrapnel has skipped underneath our table and made contact with my legs.

I experience a whirlwind of thoughts and emotions and desires. *I want out. I can't breathe. My heart is beating too fast. I have to go to the bathroom. I can't feel you, God. Are you here? Please get us out of here alive. Please! Please, please, please, please, please, God,* my mind races.

One of the gunmen says, "Who's ready to die? Who's next, huh?"

It's me. I know it's going to be me, I panic. My arms are still hanging by my side as I feel Seth hug his body closer to mine, removing any air that is between us in an attempt to brace for the bullet that is surely about to penetrate us both. *Inhale, one, two . . . exhale, one, two . . . inhale, one, two . . . exhale, one, two,* I breathe.

"Hey, you! In the white hat!" a killer hollers. I cringe as I remember that Seth has on a white baseball cap today but quickly realize they are not talking to him. In a move that will likely save his life, Seth slowly and silently slides off his white ball cap — the "jock sign" the shooters are looking for — and tucks it between us.

In the midst of this, it hits me that I haven't gotten right with God and that I'm standing on the edge of eternity even as bullets are whizzing past my head.

God, if you are real, please get me out of here alive! God, just get me out of here, and I will serve you forever. I will give you all of me and live for what really matters. Just get me out of here. God, I didn't understand before. When I was partying, I didn't get it. But it all makes sense now. I will quit the partying; I will quit the drinking; I will quit all those things. God, just get me out of here, and I will serve you. I want a second chance, God, to tell my friends, to tell my family how much I love them. I didn't get the chance to tell Dad this morning how I love him, how I care about him, and how I appreciate him. Please, please let me see my family again.

Momentarily, something that feels like peace comes in.

I don't remember needing it, hoping for it, asking explicitly for it. I remember begging to get out alive, but peace? It is an unexpected solution. And it's one that doesn't last.

I reach up with quivering fingers and take my gum out of my mouth, ignoring the lunacy of my thoughts. I tell myself that if I get shot, I certainly don't want to choke on my gum from the impact of it all.

Voices approach, and I hold my breath and strain my ears without moving my head for fear of being noticed. Someone's coming toward our table, and I dig my fingernails deeper into my already-numb palm. I hear nothing but deep voices, sneering and ridiculing.

Suddenly, Sara's voice startles me. *Surely she's not praying!* I think. *She is! She's praying out loud! What is she thinking? They'll hear her! They're going to discover us under here!*

Sara keeps whispering, her voice trembling but strong. I jab her chest with my knee hoping she will catch the hint to shut up, but she keeps going. I'm suddenly thankful for the fire alarms, desperately trusting that they will drown out my friend's ill-timed prayers.

A chair is thrust into my shoulder, and I realize that the killers' feet are inches from my head. *They're standing at our table! This is it,* I fear. *This is it!* I can sense their presence even though I can't see what's going on.

"Who's that?" he shouts as he abruptly turns around.

"John." The voice comes from the table diagonal to ours.

"Get up, John. Get out of here," the killer says soberly. "You've never done anything to us. Get out of here 'cause we're about to blow this place up. Go!"

My heart is beating so rapidly that it's not beating at all. My pulse has either flatlined or has merged itself into one long thump, I can't tell. *The library is about to be blown up, and there is no way out. I'm going to die underneath this tiny table, cowering on the floor of my own high school. I'm going to die today, and I am sixteen. I haven't even lived. And now I am going to die.* A movie of my life plays in my mind, rapid-fire images of my entire journey fluttering by.

I am lost in my despair, swimming against a tsunami of anger and confusion and fear and outrage and bitterness and resentment and grief. *Why me? Why me!* My body is shaking uncontrollably again, my eyes closed tightly as I brace for the shot that is about to hit my side.

"Hey, nerd!" one of the shooters screams at the boy under the table next to ours. My eyes nearly bug out as my body flinches instantaneously, then freezes. I wonder who they're talking to.

Then a blast of gunfire. "That'll teach him," the killer scoffs.

"I dropped my clip!" the other shooter screams.

"Look for it!" the first one shouts. "Get it, man, you've got to find it — I'm out of ammo. I've got to reload," he says, interspersing his complaint with a string of curse words.

"It's too smoky. . . . I can't see it!" comes the response.

I realize as I exhale that I've been holding my breath for what seems like hours. The voices retreat, but I hear them again within seconds. Their guns clunk down on the table directly above us as I pray desperately for God to intervene. *Make us absolutely invisible, God! Don't let them see us!*

"What the hell are we gonna do now?" one of them shouts.

My eyes are still closed as I hear metal scraping against metal — a new but equally morbid noise compared to the sounds of the previous few minutes.

"I've always wanted to kill someone with a knife," one of them says.

My stomach flips upside down as I brace for this new variation on my death. *Oh, God, I can't handle this. Please help us!*

The feet run to the other side of the library as both killers shout evil delight as they survey their damage. I hear glass shattering, something heavy crashing to the floor, then nothing.

Nothing. None of the things that threaten my life, at least.

No voices. No bombs. No gunfire. No shouting. Just fire alarms crying out with soul-stirring frequency.

Seth raises his head from beneath the table and, along with other students scattered throughout the library, races for the exit. "Let's go!" he screams.

I look up to see Seth running off with several other students. I stay prostrate on the floor, Sara gripping my legs. My mind is numb. My body is immobilized. I can't run. I can't breathe. I can't move. I have nothing.

Sara and I cling to each other in expectation of the gunmen's return to finish their job. *They've only gone to reload!* I think to myself. *They're going to be back!* In a strange way, this table has somehow become my safety zone, and I will not leave without a fight.

Seth turns around, runs back to our table, grabs my left arm, and begins dragging me out. "We have to go — NOW!" he yells, his voice strained with concern. He makes no progress with me and begins yanking on his sister. "Come on! This is our only chance!"

Awakening from a horrifying coma, Sara and I stick our legs underneath us and try to run for the exit door. My purse is strapped around my neck and is ten times its normal weight as I stabilize myself under it.

"Crystal!" Seth shouts. "Leave it! Don't take anything with you . . . just get out!"

I duck out from under my purse strap and throw it in the corner toward the computer stations as I follow Seth. *All I can see is death*, I think as I scramble over the bodies of my classmates and rush toward the exit. My legs are in slow motion, but I feel as though I'm sprinting for all I'm worth. Small fires are burning throughout the room — remnants of the killers' bombing spree. Computer monitors are smashed or shot out, and bookshelves are empty, their books strewn all over the floor. Bloody bodies lie near tables and beside computer stations, lifeless and surreal.

I reel back as the outside air hits my face, my head facing the ground, my eyes fixed on my exit path. Seth is just in front of me, Sara right behind. I finally release my gum from my fist so I can run faster. Kids are darting everywhere, some bloodied by gunshots and bomb shrapnel.

I spot a vacant police car parked on the grass just a few yards from the library's exit and rush toward it — a barricade! *Where are the killers? Where did they go?* I wonder as I hunch down by the car's tires. In the midst of the pandemonium, I crane my neck around the bumper to see what's going on.

My classmate Kasey Ruegsegger squats in front of me, her entire shoulder having been blown off from a gunshot. *I can't watch this*, I think to myself as her blood soaks the grass and dirt underneath her body. She can't muster the energy to apply pressure to her wound, so Sara crawls over to her side and pushes a piece of torn T-shirt against the blood-soaked shoulder.

Over the commotion, a kid next to me raises his voice and shouts so that we can all hear him. "There are ten guys with guns," he says. "Five on the roof. They're everywhere. Stay down. Keep ducking!"

I sidle up to the cop-car tire, realizing I am losing control. I feel a new wave of hysteria overwhelm me and sense myself entering an out-of-body experience. *This isn't happening! We're going to die. There are guys with guns . . . isn't anybody listening? Five guys on the roof with guns!* My tears are coming out in sobs and thrusts and coughs. I can't breathe. I can't cope.

Dazed, I look up to see Seth running away from the barricade toward the student parking lots. He takes cover behind a Ford Bronco just as more shots are fired in his direction. A nearby police officer raises his handgun and returns fire, aiming at the library windows on the school's second floor.

Three guys — one of whom I recognize from my class — grab me and try to calm me down. I can't function and my hands are numb, frozen claws completely incapable of movement or responsiveness. A thousand needles are pricking my fingers, hands, toes, feet. My arms are dead appendages hanging from my shoulders. I fear that if I lean on one of them, it will shatter into a million pieces.

I see a boy bleeding profusely right in front of me. He has suffered multiple gunshot wounds to his chest and legs, and everyone near him is shouting at each other to apply pressure. I scoot away from the scene, horrified by the sight of his blood. His eyes keep rolling back into his head as his friends try to save him. "My heart . . . my heart hurts," he moans. It seems he will die.

And behind that police car, on that never-ending afternoon, I die too.

I lose all functional ability and feel my facial skin fall asleep. My eyes shut out the too-bright sunlight and too-bloody sights all around me. As I heave out hysterical cries, my spine loosens, and I become a pool of nothingness. No feeling. No senses. No awareness. No comprehension. No reality. Just nothing.

I am shutting down, God. I am shutting down.

CHAPTER TWO

Why, God, Why?

"For I know the plans that I have for you," declares the LORD,
"plans for welfare and not for calamity to give you a future
and a hope."

JEREMIAH 29:11, NASB

If there were three words that plagued me after the massacre at Columbine, they were *Why, God, why?* For everyone affected that day, all that existed were questions. And eleven thousand pages of official police report later, there still were no real answers. At least not enough to outweigh the whys that plagued those of us still in the land of the living.

Minutes after my friends and I escaped from the guts of the school and crouched down beside the cop car, emergency personnel began hauling kids off, first the injured and then the rest. I was in the third carload, I remember, and they took us to the base of a nearby hill just behind the school's adjacent soccer field.

The ride was a bumpy one. So many kids were piled into the police SUV that the doors would barely shut. In the midst of being terrified that the truck wasn't safe — *Is this thing bulletproof?* — I tried to calm down. My hands wouldn't conform to my lap, they were so paralyzed. I stared at them as if they weren't my own, wondering what could possibly be happening to my body. We drove over a hill that connected the sidewalk with the soccer field, and I could have sworn the truck was going to roll over. When it finally came to a screeching halt, the doors flew open by themselves, it seemed. With intense effort, I swung my legs out of the truck's backseat to stand myself up as I tried to figure out what to do next.

I was standing below Mount Columbine — at least that's what we called it. I'd run it a thousand times for track drills, but that afternoon, it was as if I'd never been there before. Somehow, despite the masses of people around me, I felt completely and utterly alone. Even in my state of shock and disorientation, I remember thinking how odd and eerie and cold the silence was. The sky turned gray and gloomy as I tilted my head toward the clouds, clutching my grip on reality as best I could.

What just happened? Wasn't it just a few minutes ago that I was suffocated by smoke and jolted by blaring fire alarms, whizzing bullets, and friends' shrieks of terror? Were there or were there not kids running and stumbling over each other while guys were shooting at them? Weren't teachers barking orders at us? Weren't SWAT team members peppering the school with return fire? Didn't my entire life pass before my eyes underneath that stupid table?

All I knew was that for now, all was still. And all was lost. I tried desperately to wrap my mind around the magnitude of what had just happened. *Protection was gone.* I was terrified to be alone and found myself spinning slowly in place, making circles on that field, my neck jerking ahead of my body with each revolution as I heard the distant *pop-pop-pop* of ongoing gunfire. *Laughter was gone.* My trembling lips, wet with tears and numb from shock, would surely never smile again. *Optimism was gone.* Who wanted to live in a world where this sort of catastrophe could happen? There was no point in having a positive attitude. Hope was just a pipe dream — a useless way to spend my energy.

And my future was certainly gone. How would I move on from this? I stood on that little patch of overgrown field, isolated and shivering in my damp, blood-splattered clothes, no possessions with me, no people by my side, and was kept company by a single thought: *My life will never, ever be the same.*

My spinning thoughts and spinning body were abruptly stopped by a large, black microphone that had been thrust into my face, its foam covering nearly popping me in the mouth.

"What's going on in there?" The cameraman, who had evidently raced down the hill to grab an early interview, was standing just inches from my face, shouting at me as if I was beyond comprehending a normal tone of voice. "What's happening? Tell me what you saw!"

On the weed-infested field outside Columbine High School that day, with the reporter's microphone demanding some explanation from me in answer to his "What's going on in there" plea, I forced myself to wrap words around what I had seen.

"There are people with guns and they're shooting my friends!" I burst out. "So many, many people, you just don't know!" Tears streamed down my face, my smudged mascara making me look as though I'd been punched in both eyes. I had long since lost track of my jacket and wore only a tank top that was now bearing the bloody signs of war.

Suddenly, I saw Seth and Sara running toward me, seemingly from out of nowhere. Seth said we were going to head to their dad's furniture store where I could try to call my parents. I felt incapable of walking, of thinking, of staying motivated to move at all. The shock was settling into my bones. But with my friends' hands under each of my arms, we clumsily tripped our way to the store, where I finally dialed my dad's cell phone. It took me far too long to push the ten digits. My hand was numb, and my eyes kept clouding up with tears just as I tried to make out the next number's position on the dial pad. It took several tries because the phone system was so logjammed, but it finally rang through.

"Crystal?" my dad's voice cracked. He had heard the radio reports of the shooting and was overwhelmed with gratitude that I was okay. His breathing was coming in short gasps — hiccups almost — as he strained to hear my voice above the chaos in the background. "Are you okay? Where are you, Sweets? I'm on my way . . . where are you?"

"Where *were* you?" I screamed into the phone. In my confusion over the situation, I lashed out at my dad, who must have been shocked by my outburst. "Why didn't you protect me? Why didn't you save me? Where were you when I was about to be killed, Dad? Where were you!" I clenched my fists as I struggled to catch my breath between sobs.

He managed to calm me down enough to ascertain where we were, and immediately he was on his way. He finally arrived, but it felt like hours before he got to us. The traffic surrounding the school was deadlocked as police officers and parents rushed toward the scene and worried passersby rubbernecked their way down the road. Dad had been forced to park blocks away just to get to us.

I finally saw him running through the parking lot from a hundred feet off and bolted out the front door of the store, my equilibrium regained. He threw open his arms and hung on to me for dear life. I had never been hugged so tightly by another human being.

He pulled me into his chest again and stroked my hair over and over and over and over again. "I'm so sorry, Sweets, I'm so, so sorry," he kept repeating, his eyes tearing up, his voice cracking with uncustomary fear. "I'm so sorry I wasn't there. I'm so sorry."

We were told by officials on the scene that we were all supposed to complete police reports at the county library down the street, a process that was supposed to take fifteen minutes but took me well over two hours. Every time someone new stepped through the county library's front doors, my head sprung up to see who it was.

Whether he or she was a friend of mine or not, I would jump out of my chair, race to the door, and embrace whoever was standing in front of me. I was elated to see one more person alive, one more person's life spared. Plus, I couldn't seem to get my hand to write. A friend ended up writing my entire report for me as I dictated the details to him.

In the midst of the questions and hurried retelling of events, one particular officer periodically stepped onto a chair, cupped one hand over his mouth to yell over the roar of conversations going on, and recited names from a list. I couldn't tell if the names were people who were alive or students who had been killed.

I kept telling the officer that there were some people who didn't survive—that there were actually dead people inside the school at that moment. "No, sweetie, there aren't." His tone was so condescending, as if he could somehow disprove the fact that I'd stepped over dead bodies just hours ago. No one would listen to me! Was I dreaming this whole thing up?

Crisis counselors frequently presented bottles of water for me to drink, asking me to please go ahead and calm down. "Just drink a little water—it will help you feel better." Their patronizing suggestion had the opposite effect. Instead of calming me down, I grew more infuriated. Why were they acting so calm and stupid? My heart raced, my arms and legs cramped up, and my stomach threatened to revolt at any moment. It was all more than I could bear.

⬥

At some point on the evening of April 20, 1999, I stepped back inside my home on West Powers Circle. Unbelievably, it had been only twelve hours since I had raced out the door and arrived at school, physics test looming and icy wind freezing my toes.

As I walked through the entry hall and into the living room, I realized that nothing had changed, except for the half dozen people who had arrived before me. As usual, things were immaculately clean. The tall living room windows still glistened from the hot sun that always flooded them in the afternoon hours, and as I crept in toward the light, I heard the blaring vibrations of the TV anchorwoman giving blow-by-blow details of the shooting.

My mom rushed over as soon as she saw my face. Despite the fact that we'd had a rocky relationship for as long as I could remember, I hugged her tightly, grateful for the unique arrival of a mother's love. She told me that even before she received word that I was okay, she'd seen me on the news, mascara running down my face as I sobbed into the cameraman's microphone about the tragedy I'd lived through.

Suddenly, I looked down and noticed again the still-wet pools of blood soaking through my clothes. I immediately rushed upstairs to change, never wanting to see those stripes, those pants, again. My well-meaning mother told me to hand them to her so she could clean them, but I insisted that every piece of clothing on my body be thrown away. Now.

When I reemerged from my closet, our already-full house was filling up further with more friends and family members who had stopped by to check on me, as well as to learn the details of the massacre. We all sat on the couch, watching the pieced-together images on the TV while trying to figure out how the event had unfolded. I couldn't watch for very long — every sight, every sound served only to make me more upset. Plus, it seemed like people were making things up for shock value. It was infuriating.

One fact that I did absorb, however, was that the library — where I had been — had been the place worst hit during the entire siege.

Just then, my brother, Corey, pulled into the driveway. He had made the ninety-minute trip from Ft. Collins, where he attended Colorado State University, immediately upon hearing about the tragedy. I ran outside as soon as I heard he was home, and on the same driveway where he had taught me to play basketball years before, he hugged his sister with abandon — his sister who had not been murdered that day.

Later that night, *Good Morning America* called our home. They wanted to do an interview with some of the survivors — including me — in Clement Park at 4:30 the next morning. I looked at the clock on the microwave — 11:34 p.m. Afraid to fall asleep because of what I might see in my mind's eye, I lay my head in my mom's lap and repeated the story over and over again, willing myself to stay awake. I'd momentarily fall asleep but would instantly be jerked awake by memories of the bombs, the smoke, the evil laughter, the blood. My senses were besieged. Finally, at 2:30 a.m., Mom and I both slept for a whopping half hour before getting up to prepare for the interview.

I must have seemed totally scattered as I stammered through my responses, desperately trying to keep my thoughts untangled. But, despite it all, God would use my willingness to be a "talkative" survivor for a much bigger platform one day. Living through the worst school massacre in American history would miraculously usher in countless opportunities for me to be a conduit of peace and a beacon of hope in the lives of others who had suffered in similar ways. Though I couldn't possibly imagine it at the time, my bleary-eyed interview on national television that dreadful morning was to be the first step toward healing.

Nightmares

But in the immediate aftermath of the events of April 20, 1999, I knew very little peace or hope. In fact, I was tormented for more than two years by relentless nightmares every time I closed my eyes. In fitful sleep, I heard gunshots going off, bombs exploding, fire alarms raging; I felt the floor shaking and my body trembling; I tasted bitter smoke and smelled blood and death. My mind replayed the teacher's 911 call word for word and revisited the awful experience of hearing my fellow students being shot to death.

Each time I was jolted awake by the movie in my mind, I found myself in a puddle of sweat and tears, desperately wanting relief from the horror story that was now my life. More times than not, I'd dream that I was trying to run away from the sounds of guns or people shooting, but I could never make my legs work. Everyone else in the dream could move, could run, but I would be left standing still, my feet like lead weights. Everyone else in the dream found a perfect place to hide — somewhere to take shelter from the madness — but not me. I was exposed and vulnerable. Utterly defenseless.

The truth, I learned after the shooting, was that the only table in the library where not a single person was harmed was the one I was under. The dozen or so tables serving as makeshift bunkers for forty-three other students proved to be unfit protection against Dylan and Eric. At least one student hovering under each of those tables was wounded or killed at point-blank range. All in all, thirteen lives were lost, in addition to the two killers, who committed suicide.

Those killed were Matthew Kechter, a football player and straight-A student who was well-known for his endearing sense of humor and sweet smile — characteristics I saw every day in the Spanish class we shared; avid outdoorsman and aspiring Marine Corey DePooter, who would always talk fly-fishing with me, a passion of mine thanks to my dad; fifteen-year-old Daniel Mauser, who was involved in Columbine's French club; poet and songwriter Kelly Fleming; Steven Curnow, who loved soccer and at age fourteen was sure he would grow up to be a Top Gun fighter pilot; fifteen-year-old Daniel Rohrbough, who was shot while holding an exit door open for fleeing students, an expected gesture given the selflessness and thoughtfulness he was known for; Rachel Scott, a Christ-follower who was well-known, ironically, for her compassion toward anyone who didn't quite fit in — an adequate description of the gunmen themselves; John Tomlin, a devoted Christian who had spent the previous summer in Mexico building houses for the poor and was army-bound following graduation; Kyle Velasquez, who had been dubbed the "gentle giant" because of the tender spirit his large frame held; eighteen-year-olds Isaiah Shoels, who had survived two heart surgeries as a child but had mustered the strength to compete as a Columbine football player, and Lauren Townsend, who was a lover of wildlife and captain of our girls' varsity volleyball team — the team that her mother coached; and Coach Sanders, who left behind kids, grandkids, and hundreds of adoring students after serving at Columbine for twenty-five years.

And then there was Cassie.

Testimonies differ about the exact events that led to the death of Cassie Bernall, but what I do know is that my friend was senselessly shot and killed that morning in the library, just four tables away from me. One of the shooters asked her whether she believed in God, and she said, "Yes." In the moments before her death, she stood for her deepest beliefs — a reality that for years to come would cause me to question what I would have done in that situation.

But Cassie's death is hardly the point of her story. What astounded me about Cassie was her *life*. Cassie was a ray of warmth and energy for all who knew her. She chose to live — really live — each day that she was alive. Her legacy existed long before her famous death occurred, and it was one I had in many ways coveted, despite how distant it was from my lifestyle at the time.

Cassie hadn't always been so innocent — her mom candidly tells of Cassie's previous battles with smoking, drinking, and witchcraft in a book about her daughter titled, *She Said Yes* — but it was undeniable that in the last couple of years she graced this earth, she had sold out everything in order to follow Christ.

And it seemed that in the areas where Cassie stood firmly planted — her faith and her love of life — I was not so strong. Sadly, most Friday nights found me tipsy, if not drunk, at one party or another, drowning my petty frustrations about being a teenager in a cup of vodka and Coke. Cassie had "graduated" from the bad choices I was making by the time of the shooting, and somehow in her death, she taught me an important lesson about what real living is all about.

In the days following April 20, I couldn't make peace with Cassie's death. Why hadn't I been the one to die instead of her? What was God thinking? How was I supposed to live with the fact that she was killed, while I survived — wasn't she the one who was living for God? I was angry and resentful and guilt-ridden, which drove me deeper into isolation, even from people I knew and loved.

For weeks, it seemed the only people I wanted to be around were those who had been in the library with me or those who understood exactly what I had been through — like the Bernalls, Cassie's mom and dad and brother. I relished the fact that I had a place there. I belonged. I was understood and heard and cared for. I valued the fact that I was with people who had lived through the same nightmare as I had.

I will never forget walking into Cassie's room one day, long after the massacre had taken place. Her mom had finally unsealed it and allowed close friends and family members to see it just as it was when she left home for the last time. Her to-do lists were written all over her mirror with dry-erase pens; her tennis shoes and clothes were strewn across the floor. It was surreal, all these signs of life in the room of someone no longer living.

A Walking, Talking Paradox

There were many times I wished I'd also been killed so that I wouldn't have to experience the unbearable pain of living during those days. I would walk through the following minutes, days, weeks, and months with the despairing refrain of *Why, God, why?* echoing in my mind. As time marched on, I grew to loathe the confusion, the senselessness, the disruption of the far less wobbly life I once knew. There seemed to be no relief from the paralysis caused by horrifying memories, answerless questions, and the never-ending chaos that surrounded me. Then there were other times when I was solidly overjoyed that I had escaped the library that day, my body in one piece. It was as if I was becoming a walking, talking paradox.

At times I desperately needed attention and care, but other times I'd erupt in anger when someone asked a well-meaning question in an attempt to draw me out, soothe my pain, remedy my ache. I was dying a slow death, and the worst part was that I was watching it happen. I was terrified of being alone, but I hated other people's presence. I felt isolated and cold and empty, but I despised hugs and kisses and people squeezing my hand. I wrestled with my own belief in God, but I continued to beat myself up for not having been more compassionate, more loving, toward some of the kids who were killed that day. I was somehow proud of myself for having made it out alive, but I sank underneath the fact that when tragedy struck, I freaked out instead of confidently rising to the occasion. I felt entitled to grieve, but I was furious when others didn't stop their lives to grieve with me. My heart tried to comfort itself by telling me what a good friend I was to people I was close to, but my mind was assaulted by the scene of my scooting away from injured, dying classmates by that patrol car — all because I was afraid of blood.

I couldn't shake the memory of one classmate in particular lying beside me on the prickly grass, his hands and arms and legs and body stilled by shock as he begged all of us around him to stop his bleeding. Students had begun ripping off portions of their clothes in order to sop up the massive amounts of blood flowing around us. I had looked down at the piece of T-shirt someone had tossed in my direction but had done nothing with it for fear of ruining my nice clothes or catching some rare blood disease from him. Under the library table, I had felt convicted about living only for what really mattered. Yet in the backseat of the cop car that carted me away from the scene, I was paranoid about losing my sandals, my watch, my earrings.

What kind of person am I to be capable of such selfish thoughts? A walking, talking paradox. That's what I'd become.

The sky fell with surges of icy rain and gloomy snow during those days of contradiction. Fitting, I suppose, given the storm that was raging in my grieving heart.

Of course I hadn't really wanted to die. I knew I wasn't thinking clearly as I wrestled through the aftermath of Columbine. But trying to deal with such immense pain was foreign territory to me. And finding my way would prove to be the most daunting task of my life.

Back to Normal?

Classes resumed only ten brief days following the shooting, although it felt like a month had passed. To finish out the school year, Columbine students were asked to attend our rival school, Chatfield Senior High. Chatfield students would go in the morning hours, and we'd take classes in late afternoons and early evenings. I'm sure teachers and parents applauded the idea of getting all of us back into our routines, but I for one wanted to stay firmly planted in the hurt and fear and rage.

I couldn't explain the raw emotions I was feeling. "Trust God; trust Jesus," everyone would say. And so I would pray. But the truth was, nothing filled the void I felt. Church didn't. Worship songs didn't. Friends didn't. Family didn't. Pictures and newspaper clippings and other well-intended remembrances didn't. I was forever seeking something that I simply couldn't find. For me, life equated to a mounting list of whys, all directed toward this great God who was touted as caring but obviously had forgotten about those of us at Columbine.

All I knew for sure was that if I ever had to go to another funeral, it would be too soon; if I ever got out of bed, it would be a miracle; and if I ever touched one more teddy bear, one more stupid flower, I would surely throw in the towel and just give up on life. The pain was too much. The reality of my world was too overwhelming.

As time passed, I would get a little distance from the tragedy, and I'd make a hint of progress. But only nanoseconds later, another ten-ton boulder of suffering would be dropped on my head. The aftershocks of the whole experience seemed relentless. Trauma was occurring all around me and inside of me with such regularity that my definition of normal had permanently vanished.

Three Steps Forward, Two Steps Back

We can't hurry the dawn, no matter how anxiously we pace the floor or how impatiently we watch the clock. And so the question is not do we wait or not wait, because waiting is all we can do. The question is, How will we wait? Will we wait well . . . or will we wait poorly?

KEN GIRE, *THE NORTH FACE OF GOD*

Back at Columbine in the fall of 1999, everyone took stabs at normalcy, believing it was our right to "take back our school" and attend classes there as if it hadn't been a killing field just four months prior. On the first day of school, for instance, teachers, parents, and community leaders lined the parking lots leading toward the school's cafeteria doors, waving banners and cheering wildly as the students paraded back into the beloved Rebel halls. As we entered the cafeteria, a huge sign read, "Through these halls walk the finest kids in America, the students of Columbine High School!" No security guards were present, and no special systems seemed to be in place as countermeasures against future violence. Teachers hopped right back onto the hefty-homework bandwagon, believing we would all benefit from being thrust into our usual routines.

During my senior year I served as a peer counselor and saw first-hand the wrestling that went on in the hearts and minds of my class-mates. My role involved helping people who were wading through serious issues in their lives — everything from bad relationships to cutting to abuse to suicidal tendencies. Problem was, I was barely treading water myself.

Progress that year seemed so difficult to come by. A few steps forward and then *whack!* — we'd be struck with another leveling blow. Within a thirteen-month window following the shootings, our "safe and innocent" community called Littleton, Colorado, faced a laundry list of tragedies. Less than a mile from Columbine, a baby was found in the dumpster of a local retail store — he'd been tossed into the stench-filled can by his own mother and left to die an unthinkable death. Equally jarring, a high-speed chase ended with a shooting at the local Burger King. Closer to home, two Columbine freshmen who were dating were found murdered at the Subway sandwich shop where they had worked.

For those directly affected by the Columbine shootings, the nightmare wasn't over. The mother of Anne-Marie Hochhalter, one of the students who'd been paralyzed as a result of being shot at Columbine, woke up on October 22, 1999, tucked several bullets in her denim jacket pocket, and headed to the local pawn shop. She purchased a gun, meticulously loaded it with her bullets, and then shot herself in the head. Her beautiful daughter, Anne-Marie, was left alone in a permanent seat — her wheelchair — to suffer the lifelong consequences of a bipolar mother who couldn't deal with the grief of Columbine. Anne-Marie would later say that she knew her mom's motivation — strangely — was love. She didn't want her daughter to be forced to care for a sick woman when she already had her own paralysis to contend with.

Seven months later, a star basketball player at our school commit-ted suicide. Greg Barnes — a guy nearly everyone knew — had seen

Columbine's beloved teacher and athletic coach, Dave Sanders, bleed to death right in front of him one year earlier. Coach Sanders was shot by one of the gunmen while directing frantic students away from the school to save their lives. Greg must have decided that life was simply too much to take. He hung himself in his garage, and his father found him later that morning.

I couldn't make sense of everything that had happened; I couldn't make sense of why I was still alive; I couldn't make sense of what was now my reality. Children from schools in various states sent cards and letters expressing their sadness over what we at Columbine had gone through. I still have one letter from a seven-year-old named Chelsea that says, "To Columbine High School. I'm sorry. It probably was scary." Strangely, perhaps, her simple sentiment meant so much more to me than the comments from the many people who hopelessly tried to make everything add up.

Truth was, nothing added up. Nothing made sense. And it likely never would. I was utterly baffled by the turn life had taken, and I told God regularly that I didn't know if I'd ever trust him again. Yet in the same breath I would often cry out to him like a small, frightened child, because I doubted there was anyone else who could possibly help me find a reason to keep on living.

"How Are You *Really* Doing, Crystal?"

Author Anne Lamott once wrote of her battle trying to overcome an eating disorder in her clever and profound book on faith, *Traveling Mercies*. Eventually spiraling into a pit of despair, Lamott broke down and called a specialist she thought could help. Cranky and skeptical, she viewed the specialist's advice as nonsense — the suggestions included futile things like calling a friend immediately after eating a meal simply to wedge a little time between the meal and Lamott's typical postmeal practice of purging everything she'd just eaten.

During one therapy session several weeks into her treatment, Rita, the specialist, wasted no time probing Lamott's eating patterns so far that day. Their comments butted up against each other, more defensive hostility than friendly chatter.

"What did you have for breakfast?" Rita began.

"Cereal, of course."

"And were you hungry when you ate it?"

"What do you mean?"

"I mean, did you experience hunger, and then make breakfast?"

"I don't really understand what you're asking."

"Let me put it this way. Why did you have breakfast?"

"Oh, I see. I had breakfast because it was breakfast time."

"But were you hungry?"

"Is this a trick question?"

The process of learning to properly feed herself was completely baffling to Anne Lamott. She describes the first week that she was tasked with eating *only* when she was hungry:

> My assignment was to notice what it *felt* like when I was hungry. It was so strange. I was once again the world's oldest toddler. I walked around peering down as if to look inside my stomach, as if it was one of those old-fashioned front-loading washing machines with a window through which you could see the soapy water swirling your clothes. And I paid attention until I was able to isolate this feeling in my stomach, a gritchy kind of emptiness, like a rat was scratching at the door, waiting to be let in.[1]

Are you really hungry? The question was the bane of Anne's existence for months as she sought freedom from the bondage of bulimia. And I could relate, albeit on much different terms.

"How are you *really* doing, Crystal?" everyone would ask in the days and weeks following Columbine. Soon enough, I realized that the question was just a kinder, gentler way for people to ask, "Aren't you any better yet?" There was an indictment there, beneath that caring-question veil. And while their appropriate desire was to see me transformed back into the Crystal they once knew and loved, I wasn't ready — would I ever be? — to stare at my heart the way Lamott had stared at her stomach, asking it, "Yes, but are you really any better?" The answer my heart would surely give just made me cringe.

I was so despondent for days on end that I refused to eat. The grief was simply too heavy. Eventually friends of mine force-fed Girl Scout Thin Mint cookies to me, one after another after another. It seemed to be the only thing I could choke down.

During the three months when the school library windows were boarded up, the bloodstained carpets pulled up, and all of the memorial services held, I desperately wanted to disappear. The "how are you doing?" question everyone felt compelled to ask me on a daily basis — and on bad days several times an hour — was the primary catalyst for my desired vanishing act.

Learning to heal myself — the way Anne Lamott had to learn to feed herself — would take courage and strength and resolve, none of which I had at the time. And in my heart of hearts, I knew the healing wouldn't ultimately come from me anyway, but from God. After dancing to my own drumbeat for so many years, was I finally ready to face him?

Childhood Anguish

I'm not sure young children can see dysfunction in the lives of their parents for what it is. To some extent, their home life is simply all they know. This was true for my brother and me — was there really such a thing as *normal*, anyway? It wasn't until my early teenage years that the puzzle pieces started fitting together.

For a portion of my life, Mom did PR for a linen supplier to restaurants and hotels. She made frequent calls to various clients around the Denver metro area, but by the time my brother and I were home from school each day, she'd typically be back. Most late afternoons and evenings found Mom in the kitchen, preparing some delicious meal that we'd all scarf down before heading our separate ways. But one thing was always true: She'd have a full glass of wine in hand and plenty more in the refrigerator.

At first, my young mind just thought she drank slowly. How was I supposed to know something was amiss? She kept a neat house. She was a great cook — fantastic smells that originated in the kitchen were always floating through our house. And she definitely cared about our family. But looking back, I realize that I hardly ever saw her drink anything but wine. As alcohol became her steady companion, she and I grew even further apart, and the atmosphere in our home became increasingly hostile and volatile.

My dad, although undeniably enraged by my mom's addiction, had his own issues with alcohol. For years, I remember thinking he was just a very tired man. After all, he owned his own landscaping company and on most days would put in twelve hours in the hot sun before coming home to tackle household chores or lawn work in our own yard. By the time I saw him each evening, he was beat.

What I didn't know until much later was that he would start planning his drinking escapades on his way home from work every day. Knowing he would be walking into a war zone with my mom, he'd figure out exactly how much whiskey he'd have to drink in order to avoid dealing with her. He'd conk out by ten every night, a massive snoring machine vibrating on top of one of the comfy couches in our living room. But strangely, despite his disengagement on many occasions, I knew he still cared. I knew his love for me was real. And I was definitely a "daddy's girl."

While I'm sure Mom and Dad found moments of enjoyment, throughout the majority of my life I don't remember seeing them behave affectionately toward each other. To me, it seemed like they simply existed under the same roof — there was no obvious love there. By the time I was a preteen, the pattern in our home was set: As the sun went down, Mom's and Dad's voices went up. I remember nights when I'd be trying to fall asleep but would be jarred by the sound of their screaming at the top of their lungs. They never knew it, but I'd scream too, as loud as I could, to make them stop. Of course they never heard me, and they never stopped.

It wasn't until I was a freshman in college that my parents finally separated. Their divorce became final three years later.

I don't remember exactly how my own drinking started, but I know that early in my high school years it got hold of me and wouldn't let go. During my eighth grade year, I had prayed the prayer asking Christ to come into my life. And I meant it, as far as I could tell. I remember kneeling beside my bed at my maternal grandmother's house — my brother, cousins, and I have always called her Gam — and listening intently as she described all that it meant to be a Christian. It was all so purposeful and important to her, and I coveted the peace and steadiness I saw in her life. She was far from perfect, but she was the most caring, loving, life-giving person I'd ever known. I wanted to know God the way she did, and I went to church regularly, seeking the personal relationship with Jesus that gave Gam so much joy and peace.

As my freshman year of high school unfolded, however, I faced an increasingly challenging dilemma. On one hand, I was hanging on to my freshly minted commitment to following Christ, but on the other hand, I began craving all that the world had to offer. And in record time, I found myself willing to do whatever it took to grab hold of the popularity, the achievement, the "coolness" that I saw in other people at my school.

It didn't take me long to realize that the fast track to the "in" crowd involved attending weekend parties. Guys only noticed girls who partied, and so I determined that the only way for me to become the popular person I wanted to be was to show my face every weekend, no matter what. I saw the girls that guys in my school liked, and they were all impeccably dressed and successful and beautiful — or at least what I thought beauty was at the time. I wanted so badly to be friends with them all. I wanted the lives they had — lives that seemed so much better than my own.

I remember the first party I went to in high school. The girl who invited me was a good friend in my church youth group, so I thought nothing about saying yes. *I'll just go to the party and tell everyone about Jesus,* I told myself. *I'll be a good witness — never mind that they'll all be so drunk they won't understand a word I'm saying.* I genuinely thought I could hang on to my convictions while being hip-deep in the teen partying scene.

I should have known better.

Instead of my having a good impact on it, my new environment influenced me — for the worse. As the downward spiral started, though, I still cared a lot about what people thought. I cared about what my athletic coaches thought. I cared about what my friends thought. I cared, most of all, about what my dad thought. I was an incurable people-pleaser, and I knew it.

So there was this delicate balance I tried to maintain. I'd get sloshed, but I'd do it in a "careful" sort of way. Putting so much stock in other people's opinions was likely the thing that kept me from taking a nosedive off the edge of reason on more than one occasion.

The thought of soiling my reputation in front of all those "important" people absolutely terrified me.

I began to have "just one" at each party. In my estimation, drinking made me a much more fun person and allowed me — otherwise a fairly shy girl — to open up. My defenses would fall away at parties, and a more outgoing version of me showed up time and time again. Finally! I could be in a social setting without feeling like a complete idiot.

Over time, the allure of the party scene sort of overshadowed my healthy paranoia regarding everyone's opinion. One drink at one party once in a while eventually turned into several drinks at several parties every weekend. But I rationalized things by partying with the girls I was playing sports with. (At least if I got in trouble, they'd go down with me.)

By the start of my junior year, in one night's time I could easily put down a whole bottle of anything — vodka, rum, you name it — as long as I had something like Coke or juice to chase it with.

Eventually, my drinking escalated even further. My friends and I would find our way into a few bottles of liquor before parties and would get tipsy before we even left the house to go out. Typically, I'd save my lunch money during the week — a few bucks a day courtesy of my dad — and then pay someone off at the end of the week to purchase the booze for us. Vodka won out as my drink of choice because it was so easy to conceal — we'd mix it with juice and carry it in a Snapple bottle, a juice bottle, whatever, so that it just looked like a normal drink.

During those days, I made some unbelievable decisions. I'd drive my car when I was extremely drunk (I rationalized it by saying that I was more alert when I was drunk than when I was sober). I'd get drunk the night before an early-morning sports practice. I once even jumped out of a moving car thinking it would be fun. All of this in the name of being cool. But to this day, I believe that each time I got home, I'd desperately hope to get caught so that I could be rescued from my "cool" life.

Stuck in Average

Drinking helped me wipe away the issues of my day — just as my parents had modeled for me. The "severe stuff" of my life as a teenager — a bad grade on a quiz, a fight with my mom, whatever — simply dissolved into thin air as I guzzled more and more alcohol. I pulled out of other, suddenly less important endeavors like church and all that it had meant to me in terms of seeking a meaningful relationship with God. My friends, my boyfriend, my routine — all fell by the wayside since they didn't fit in with my new social schedule. *If they won't party with me, that's their loss*, I'd tell myself.

After I'd developed a new, livelier circle of friends, I started having parties at my house. It was all so perfect: My mom would buy my booze, and sometimes she'd hang around for the parties themselves. My dad probably wouldn't have approved, but he was often sleeping or passed out when they occurred.

My friends and I would hang out in the hot tub and drink with the explicit purpose of getting drunk. But unfortunately, once you're drunk, you tend to make less than terrific decisions. Guys had finally started noticing me, which I guess was the ultimate goal in my becoming-popular plan. Even then, though, I felt like I was stuck in average. I couldn't seem to get the "best" — the most handsome guy, the most popular one, the strongest athlete. I never felt good enough or pretty enough, which caused me to plummet further into behavior that reflected my lack of self-respect.

Sexually, things began innocently enough with kissing one guy or another, but the progression to worse trends was inevitable. Looking back, I wasn't prepared for the toll it would take on my heart to so willingly — so thoughtlessly — give another piece of my soul away weekend after weekend.

I'd let things progress to a certain point with one guy, stopping when I felt sleazy about what I was doing. (Of course, when I was drinking, all bets were off. All inhibitions were gone, and any convictions that tried to sneak up on me were instantly brushed aside.) But the next time, with the next guy, getting to that same level carried with it no shame whatsoever. And so I'd go further.

Much like ripping a Band-Aid off the same bloody wound day after day, you eventually get numb to it all.

I despise that season of my past — the drunkenness and carelessness and selfishness of it all. Didn't I want to be a "good kid"? Didn't I want to be safe and responsible and respected? The truth was, I did. But I also wanted desperately to be accepted. To be liked. To be "in." The longer I walked that tightrope, the more I realized that at some point, I'd have to fall to one side or the other.

In January of 1999, I scaled back on the partying, but I couldn't bring myself to stop cold. It had become too much a part of me — to quit altogether would have been like chopping off my right arm. And, realistically, I still wanted (needed, even) to hang out with my partying friends, to be a part of their lives and get updates on what was going on from the people who were in the know.

It seemed I'd become perilously trapped on the tightrope, every step a tenuous one as I tried to balance all of the Crystals I wanted to be. I had made a decision to follow Christ, but Christian Crystal just didn't have the sex appeal I'd hoped to have. I'd given sports my blood, sweat, and tears, but All-Star Crystal was someone I'd never meet. Despite countless hours slaving away over textbooks, Academic Crystal couldn't keep up. I coveted being part of the beautiful crowd, but Popular Crystal only showed up when I was tipsy or flat-out drunk. And Good-Girl Crystal never had any fun.

Feeling disillusioned by how empty the "good life" I was living really was, I knew something had to shift. Dramatically so. But where was I supposed to start? I felt sure that the Jesus I had committed myself to as an eighth grader was probably so disappointed with the course I'd taken that he would never want me back. I hated who I had become. But I felt helpless to do anything about it.

Glimmers of Hope

After the shootings happened at Columbine, life just seemed to be a cruel joke at best. But as the months went by, something in my soul kept telling me differently.

I felt like I had been dropped in a dense forest, the sunset making the shadows long and the path difficult to see. I would catch sight of a minute morsel, a little crumb of clarity on the ground at my feet. And so I would walk that way for a few steps until I would get disoriented again. I'd peek down at my shoes, hoping for another clarity crumb, and sure enough, there it would sit. Nothing grand. No neon lights or voices from heaven or wild supernatural tugs in one direction or another. Just a dose of understanding and revelation that would be enough to prompt me to put one foot in front of the other for one more minute, hour, day, week.

I began to long for God again, even though I was angry and bewildered over all that he had allowed to happen in my life. *Maybe*, I thought, *just maybe, the relationship with Jesus I began pursuing as a preteen is the answer to the deepest questions and cries of my heart.*

As my graduation from Columbine High School came and went, I wanted to remember the summer after I graduated for something other than sitting by a pool or being tempted to hit parties every night. I called a friend of mine who had said that if I were ever interested in making a difference in someone's life, he could make all the arrangements for me to work with a ministry called Samaritan's Purse. (I had already been on a trip with them to provide relief in war-torn Kosova only eight months after the shootings at Columbine. And they were the same folks I would go to Russia with five years later.) For more than twenty years, Samaritan's Purse had been deploying long-term teams all over the place — in Kenya, Rwanda, Bangladesh, Egypt, Papua New Guinea, Haiti, and Ecuador, to name a few — in order to first provide much-needed physical attention and then much-more-needed spiritual healing to people who had been struck by disaster and ravished by famine and disease. "Heal the sick who are there and tell them, 'The kingdom of God is near you,'" Jesus said in Luke 10:9. Samaritan's Purse had taken Christ's commission seriously.

"Where can you send me?" was the question I posed when I called my friend in the summer of 2000.

Honduras was the answer.

I would be working with a group conducting rebuilding efforts following a massive hurricane that had swept the region. Specifically, I'd be part of the water purification team, responsible for building cement water purifiers that would provide clean water for families who were desperately in need of it. We would mix cement by hand and then pour it into giant molds, pounding out all the air bubbles so it would set properly. It was so unlike anything I'd ever done before, but I relished how noble the endeavor felt.

At the end of every day, I'd be covered from head to toe in cement, and my fingers would be swollen with blisters. But it was intriguing to me that my work produced immediate fruit. As the sun set each evening, I could literally look out over the plot of land we'd worked and see filter after filter ready to be delivered to people who needed clean water.

That summer proved to be harder emotionally than I could have imagined. I plumbed new depths of pain and grief. I'd run two miles every morning, walk another two, and often run again each afternoon — all in an attempt to relieve the stress I was feeling. But it didn't work. By the end of the summer, I had gained twenty-five pounds; my face, chest, and back were broken out with acne; and emotionally I was a wreck. I genuinely believed that no one liked me, cared about me, or was there to support me.

The God I had so often pushed away was now the only hope I had for survival. I began begging him to replace the horrific scenes that were running in my mind and heart with his peace and assurance and presence. I prayed the only thing I knew to pray: that understanding would replace my confusion, that confidence would replace my fear, that comfort would replace my loneliness.

I want so badly to lay my problems and worries at the foot of your cross, God. If there is any possible way to redeem all that has happened in my life for good, please do it. Use all that has happened to me to touch other people. Shine through me and keep Satan away from my life. Please don't allow him to use anything against me. Instead, I hope that you alone can be glorified in my messed-up life.

The Beginning of Healing

Just days later, I realized that God had begun to answer my prayer. I was given the opportunity to accompany Cassie Bernall's mom, Misty, to a very special orphanage near Tegucigalpa. She had e-mailed me earlier in the summer to say she would be making a trip to Honduras — would I like to join her for the weekend?

When I arrived at the beautiful yellow and white building where she was waiting for me, I found the peace and assurance and evidence of God's presence I had been longing for all summer in the eyes of one familiar face. Misty Bernall and I hugged for what felt like an eternity before turning to enter the building.

As we looked up at the sign boasting the name of the orphanage, both of us swelled with pride. The name read,

> Hogar de Niños
> Cassie René Bernall
> Home for Children

Proudly displayed on the front lawn was a large memorial wall — a permanent reminder of Cassie's life and legacy. I traced the raised bronze letters with my finger as I read the inscription beneath the bronze-cast picture of my long-lost friend.

> Bien Hecho, Buen y Fiel Siervo
> Well Done, Good and Faithful Servant

Este hogar es dedicado	This home is dedicated
en memoria de	in memory of
CASSIE RENÉ BERNALL	CASSIE RENÉ BERNALL

ELLA	SHE
DIJO	SAID
"SÍ"	"YES"

Fue muerta por su valentía	She was killed for her courage and
fidelidad al Señor. Ese día, ella	her faithfulness to the Lord. That
entro a la Gloria recibiendo la	day, she entered Glory receiving the
CORONA DE LA VIDA	CROWN OF LIFE

| NACIO EL 6 DE NOV. 1981 | BORN NOV. 6, 1981 |
| FALLECIO EL 20 DE ABRIL 1999 | DIED APRIL 20, 1999 |

ESTE HOGAR ES HECHO	THIS HOME IS RAISED
CON AMOR POR SUS	IN LOVE BY HER
PADRES MISTY Y BRAD,	PARENTS, MISTY AND
SU HERMANO CHRIS, SU	BRAD, HER BROTHER
FAMILIA Y HERMANOS	CHRIS, AND HER FAMILY
EN CRISTO. HASTA QUE	AND BROTHERS IN
NOS REUNAMOS EN	CHRIST. UNTIL WE
EL PARAISO.	MEET IN PARADISE.

DEDICADO EL 20 DE ABRIL 2000

DEDICATED 20 APRIL 2000

In his book *Searching for God Knows What*, Donald Miller says that "the most important thing you can do is love your kids, hold them and tell them you love them because, until we get to heaven, all we can do is hold our palms over the wounds."[2]

Hold our palms over the wounds. Yes, that is what I'm beginning to experience. Although I still couldn't make sense of everything that had happened in my life so far, I began to realize that nervously glancing in the rearview mirror would never heal me. No, the greatest aid would be gazing into the horizon that was waving me toward itself through my windshield. Until that point, my neck had been craned around, looking behind me for so long that I didn't realize anything even existed in front of my face. But suddenly, I realized that *hope* was what I was catching glimmers of up ahead, and I could choose its healing power if I so desired.

As I stood before the orphanage memorial, Misty Bernall's delicate hand in mine, our palms resolving to gently hold and cover our deep wounds, I looked down at my chest and silently asked my heart, *Aren't you any better yet?*

Finally the answer, although tentative, was yes.

CHAPTER FOUR

The Upside of Suffering

The Spirit of the Lord GOD is upon me,
Because the LORD has anointed me
To bring good news to the afflicted;
He has sent me to bind up the brokenhearted,
To proclaim liberty to captives
And freedom to prisoners;
To proclaim the favorable year of the LORD
And the day of vengeance of our God;
To comfort all who mourn,
To grant those who mourn in Zion,
Giving them a garland instead of ashes,
The oil of gladness instead of mourning,
The mantle of praise instead of a spirit of fainting.
So they will be called oaks of righteousness,
The planting of the LORD, that He may be glorified.
ISAIAH 61:1-3, NASB

Some of my fondest memories are of days gone by when I'd watch my dad work in the yard for hours on end. Although he'd been the owner of his own landscaping business since he was thirty, it was always more than just his livelihood — it was his passion-pursuit as well. Kind of a plant junkie. Thanks to my dad, and contrary to the proverbial cobbler's-children-never-having-shoes dilemma, our yard looked beautiful every day of the year. (And given Colorado's infamously stubborn soil, this was a monumental feat.) I never caught the bug, but I respected his outdoor prowess anyway.

Dad probably would know how to pronounce *Aquilegia canadensis*, but don't ask me to. It's Latin for "wild columbine," a resilient and independent purple and white blossom that self-seeds and pops up, uninvited, in the most surprising of places. I guess that qualifies it as a weed. But it's a beautiful and stunning weed, so most people don't call it that.

Regardless, the lavender and white columbine was adopted as Colorado's official state flower sometime in the late nineteenth century. Simple. Beautiful. And protected. Maybe that's why it is known to freely throw its seed around, the wind's parameters its only restriction. It is *protected*. Safe and secure and sheltered.

Or maybe not. While it's generally accepted by natives that the state flower shouldn't be picked, the law forbidding it simply doesn't exist. Sure, maybe the flower believed all along that it was protected, thinking, *People won't pick me — I'm the state flower!* But in reality, it was just as vulnerable as those of us who were once students at its namesake school, Columbine High. We found out the hard way that the protection we so blindly and confidently depended on never really existed at all.

A few weeks after the shootings, when I was already life weary and disillusioned by the tender age of sixteen, the columbine flower became a symbol for me of persevering in the face of vulnerability. My family all looked on as my dad and I stood in our large backyard on a swelteringly hot summer afternoon, decked out with gardening gloves and grieving hearts, to accomplish a mission. The mission involved stuffing thirteen columbine flower plants into the dark soil in our well-tended beds to represent thirteen lives senselessly lost.

We covered the last of the thirteen seedlings and stood beside each other in silence for a few minutes, reflecting on the event that brought us to that occasion. My mind trailed off to the idea of sowing and reaping. It was a miracle, really, how anything could grow. You stick a few seedlings down into dirt and then step back to watch. Minutes tick by. Nothing. You realize you've been standing out there baking in the sun for an hour. Still nothing. Day turns to night, and night turns to day again. The dew dries as the earth heats up, and you're still standing there, staring at a mysterious black mound of soil. *Where's the flower?* you wonder. *How long is this going to take, anyway?*

It occurred to me that hope is the acknowledgment that despite the deplorable conditions that caused us to put those particular plants in the ground — they were, after all, the remembrance of my murdered friends — those fragile columbine seedlings would in fact spring up from the dirt one day and fully grow into the stunning purpose for which they were created: to be colorful, life-giving manifestations of God's creative beauty-from-ashes promise. And to remove the dirty process of putting down roots and elbowing their way up to full height would be to jeopardize the flowers' strength to stand in the face of cruel elements like wind and rain and hail and stray dogs. Their hope for beauty existed only because they were willing to endure the suffering first.

Howard Hendricks, renowned professor at Dallas Theological Seminary, says that while we're alive on earth, we are actually living in the land of the *dying*, not the land of the living.[1] As difficult as that is to get our arms around, we have to remember that we were not built for this world but instead for eternity — for an everlasting reality that includes God's ever-present power and perfection.

Suffering's End Game

These days, my favorite Bible looks like it's been windblown, sat on, run over, and tossed in the spin cycle a few times — kind of like my life over the past seven years. It's an old NIV, no bigger than my two hands one on top of the other, and it's entirely covered with a collage of friends' pictures and those miniature cards boasting religious clichés they sell beside cash registers at Christian bookstores. Every card, every photo — they all mean something to me, which is why this particular Bible is my favorite.

The wear and tear has taken a toll. Many of the charts, maps, and concordance pages have come loose from the binding, but I keep them stuffed in there out of respect. It may not be pretty, but it reminds me of the rough-and-tumble journey I've been on, learning and living by God's Word — or trying to, at least.

A quick thumb through of the pages that are still attached would tell even the casual observer that I'm no Old Testament scholar. You get to the book of Matthew, though, and all bets are off. From the Gospels through Revelation, it's tough to find any white space at all. Every margin, every column separator, every inch between the text and the footnotes are covered with my own feeble ponderings.

Sometimes the jots are helpful explanations from Bible teachers of the verses above or below or beside. Other times my scribblings are intended to reflect, through a short prayer, my deep desire to live out the verse. In the margin of Luke 6:37, which encourages us not to judge and not to condemn, it reads, "Lord, forgive me for my critical spirit and my judgmental heart. Let me love . . . and worry about my *own* sin."

Still other places show expressions of sheer excitement over some new revelation. For instance, every verse in Ephesians 3 is overtaken by four bold-faced words, "Live a worthy life!" And every time I turn to that page, my heart constricts as it sees the command in my own handwriting. *Is my life really worthy of* anything *right now?* I have to ask myself with each encounter. It injures my ego every time, but it gets me refocused immediately.

There are passages that I can hardly read, they are so slathered by ink. And it all looks very holy, very spiritual, all those written-down convictions, as if I've arrived or have got the righteous-living thing down.

In reality, though, the scribbles simply force my me-centered self to sit up and take notice of the life Christ wants me to live. They remind me that this life is not my own. That the be-all and end-all of my existence is to pursue *God's* purposes rather than my own. And that sometimes his purposes aren't as obvious as I'd wish.

About a year after Columbine, a set of verses so captivated me that I committed them to memory. They show up in Psalm 139 and breathe life into my heart and mind each and every time I read them.

> For you created my inmost being;
>   you knit me together in my mother's womb.
> I praise you because I am fearfully
>   and wonderfully made;
>   your works are wonderful,
>   I know that full well.
> My frame was not hidden from you
>   when I was made in the secret place.
> When I was woven together in the depths of the
>   earth, your eyes saw my unformed body.
> All the days ordained for me were written in your
>   book before one of them came to be.
>   (verses 13-16)

The part about me being fearfully and wonderfully made has always stopped me in my tracks because I certainly don't always feel wonderful exactly as God made me. But that's not the part that has stumped me most. Where I get sidelined is on the psalmist's sentiment there on the fourth line that says God's *works* are wonderful too. I mean, if he's in charge of everything, and all of his works are wonderful, then how does suffering ever wedge its way into the equation? The question baffled me so profoundly that I felt compelled to launch an all-out search mission for some answers.

Immediately following Columbine, I'd started turning to Scripture for answers. But it was more defensive than offensive — a way to feel his peace and his presence when I was having a down day. It wasn't until nearly a year later that I mustered the courage to come to God with my hard questions. How comforting it was to find his Word unfailing in its ability to teach me, grow me up, and encourage me for the journey ahead!

Purpose in Paradox

If there is one set of verses in my tattered Bible that wins the award for the most underlines, asterisks, and exclamation points, it is Romans 5:2-5. For me, this passage holds out great hope in the clues it gives to some of Scripture's most profound paradoxes — particularly the dilemma of how a good God could let horrible things happen to people he claims to love. The "suffering dilemma" was one I was all too familiar with and desperately needed to come to some kind of truce with if I was ever to climb out of fear and cynicism. In this passage we read, "But we also rejoice in our sufferings, because we know that suffering produces perseverance; perseverance, character; and character, *hope*. And hope does not disappoint us, because God has poured out his love into our hearts by the Holy Spirit, whom he has given us" (emphasis mine).

Obviously, I was not alone in wondering what possible good could come from suffering if Paul had to spell it out for the believers in Rome. I highlighted those verses like crazy, not because they reflected how I was already living but because they reflected how I earnestly *wanted* to live. I truly wanted to view affliction as a conduit for all those great things; it's just that my first response never seemed to cooperate with the verses' suggestion. Throughout my teen years, each time I faced suffering I tended to have every reaction known to man *except*, "Yes! Thank you, God, for this pain, this anguish, this affliction! This will eventually lead to hope, I just know it!"

But Scripture says that there really *can* be joy in the midst of affliction. Maybe it's not the jump-up-and-down, shouts-of-jubilation kind of rejoicing, but it is joy nonetheless.

When we make peace with God through the grace that is ours only because of Jesus — that is, when we ask Jesus to come into our life and take control instead of relying on our own street smarts and insight to navigate our life — then we can rejoice, verse 2 says, at the *hope* of the glory of God. Meaning, we can have hope because we have the greatest possible destiny to look forward to: an eternity spent by our Creator's side.

Interestingly, this same word *rejoice* is found in verse 3 as well. Exact same impossible-to-pronounce Greek word, *kauchaŏmai*, which means "to boast." But this time, rather than talking about how we should respond to the promise of a fantastic future with God, it's suggesting that this be our response to the *suffering* that we face between now and then. So we are supposed to boast in the midst of our sufferings.

But boast about what?

The four verses I focused on in Romans 5 are tucked inside a broader context: Paul is telling the Roman church about the primary benefits to having faith in the gospel message. In other words, what good does it do a person to believe the message of Christ?

"Glad you asked," Paul says, as he rattles off a list of seven benefits, things like peace and access to God and eternal security in Christ — and finding joy in suffering. So in essence, the ability to rejoice in the face of suffering was viewed as a positive byproduct of the Christ-following life. And what Paul wrote centuries ago is just as true today: Suffering with joy is a *primary benefit* of being a Christian.

After Columbine, as weeks turned into months and into years, my greatest desire became to trade in my familiar, faith-deflating thoughts and beliefs for this one spectacular paradox: Affliction really *can* hold hands with joy. This seemed like wishful thinking rather than truth to me, but somehow I knew that if I couldn't latch on to it, I would never climb out of the pit, much less find any purpose or passion to make life worth getting up for every day.

Specifically, I realized that if I was going to view suffering as something worthwhile, I'd have to discover some pretty stellar by-products of it that would help shift my "suffering sucks" paradigm to something a little more optimistic. As I look back now on all of my experiences — the seasons of suffering as well as the steps of progress I've made — I'm coming to see more clearly that Paul wasn't just preaching or blowing smoke. He had come to believe *from his own personal experience*, which included plenty of suffering, the *truth* of what he was proclaiming with such conviction to the Romans. He could encourage them to do something so contrary to human nature — rejoice in the midst of their pain — because he himself had learned that there were by-products of suffering worth rejoicing over.

As I continued to ask God to help me see my own life through the eyes of such faith and conviction, everything kind of came together. All at once, I was learning what it looked like to experience perseverance of spirit, strength of character, and the kind of hope that really did defy human reasoning. And I even began to be grateful for the hidden spiritual blessings that suffering could deposit in my life if I was willing to experience it with less kicking and screaming.

Along with the gifts of perseverance, character, and hope that Paul promised the Romans, I discovered for myself at least three related "benefits" of human pain. Deeper intimacy with God was high on the list. A healthier perspective on life was a much-needed and invaluable gift. And perhaps the ultimate treasure of all was the most unexpected in my own life: a closer resemblance to Christ himself through the kind of transformation that only suffering can produce.

Just to Be with You

The first by-product I noticed from the suffering I had walked through was a closer relationship with God. Because I so desperately needed a new foundation of hope and joy in the midst of my brokenness, I continued to scour God's Word for clues about how to build these crucial intangibles into my soul. Regarding hope, Psalm 62 says that it can be found only in God:

> My soul, wait in silence for God only,
> For my hope is from Him.
> He only is my rock and my salvation,
> My stronghold; I shall not be shaken.
> (verses 5-6, NASB)

Since hope comes from God alone, as we draw near to hope, by definition we also draw near to the hope-Giver himself. This is the unexpected reality of suffering — God knows that in order to experience relief from our pain, we will have to draw closer to him.

During the Easter season last year I had the privilege of seeing *The Thorn*, a two-hour dramatic representation of the life and ministry of Christ, at New Life Church in Colorado Springs, Colorado. It was the production's tenth anniversary, and in that week alone, more than fifty thousand people saw one of eight performances, and well over four thousand people made first-time professions of faith at the end of those nights.

Without a doubt, the most powerful — if not utterly gut wrenching — part of the entire performance was the crucifixion scene. In *The Thorn's* portrayal, Jesus was chained to a stake at center stage,

Roman guards and mockers surrounding him as he was beaten to a pulp. Literally.

The torture continued as Jesus silently swayed back and forth, his body completely at the mercy of the whip's motion. The voice of Satan could be heard above the throbbing crowd as he taunted the King of kings. "Walk away," Satan hissed. "Haven't you endured enough, Jesus?" His calculated pronunciation of Christ's name was loaded with ridicule as he slithered across the ground.

His arms still chained above his head to the stake that stood tall behind him, Jesus gasped for faint wisps of air, lifting up on his toes so he could lower his arms toward his torso and allow oxygen into his lungs. The thrusting lashes across his back continued, his gashes blowing open further to expose raw skin, fresh blood. The jeering crowd grew louder, shouting degrading religious slurs as Roman guards unchained Jesus and let him fall to the ground in a bloody heap.

The guards hauled him up by his underarms, insisting that he stay standing under the weight of his own impossibly heavy cross. It would serve as the agent of his death, and he was commanded to bear it himself as he stumbled down the *Via Dolorosa* (literally, the "way of suffering").

As he took those first few painful steps, I heard the slow, beautiful strains of a song I knew well. Originally recorded by the Christian band Third Day, it is titled "Love Song." The song's powerful lyrics echoed throughout the auditorium as Jesus labored to take each step. Lash marks on his back and sides and arms were wet with blood. His hair was matted down, sweaty and bloody from the one-sided battle. I looked into his eyes as he stumbled by my section and saw deep pain register in them as he stared out at the abusive crowd — the crowd that was full of the same people he loved.

Angry soldiers kept pulling him up when he would fall down, insisting he complete the walk to the cross. Finally, the procession arrived at Golgotha ("the place of the skull"), and they nailed him to the crossbar before dropping it into the ground. Writhing in pain as he hung there, Jesus rolled his back and flexed in agony. A piercing crown of thorns was thrust on his head as tears and sweat dripped from his brow.

Disciples and family members looked on as he suffered, wrenched by unbelievable pain and torment. *"Eloi, Eloi, lama sabachthani?"* Jesus cried to God, "My God, my God, why have you forsaken me?" (Mark 15:34). His head fell to his chest, his lungs releasing their final breath as the final words of the song faded away.

The auditorium was filled with more than seven thousand people, but you could have heard a pin drop at that moment. Seconds later, the skies erupted in thunderous claps and flashes of bright lightning before the entire world went completely black.

A cappella voices quietly began singing, "What can wash away my sin? Nothing but the blood of Jesus." Satan slithered at the foot of the cross, his eyes fixed on Jesus' lifeless body, as the voices continued. "What can make me whole again? Nothing but the blood of Jesus. Oh, precious is the flow that makes me white as snow. No other fount I know, nothing but the blood of Jesus."[2] Mother Mary, mother of Jesus, sobbed as the old spiritual came to a close.

Just to be with you. The phrase crept into the recesses of my heart and captivated my attention. Just to be with you, child, I'd do anything. Just to be with you, average one, there's no price I wouldn't pay. Just to be with you, lonely one, there's nothing I wouldn't do. Just to be with you, distracted one, I would climb any mountain. Just to be with you, disrespectful one, I promise I would go to any length. Just to be with you, suffering one, I would give my life away.

This is the stunning truth of the gospel. Just to be with us, Christ gave everything that he could possibly give, even his very life on a criminal's cross. The Bible says that every single one of us has fallen short of God's perfect standard and is therefore separated from him (see Romans 3:23). But instead of making us figure out a way to gain access to God, he provided a bridge — his Son, Jesus Christ. Sent to earth in flesh and bones, Jesus was born to die for me. For you. For the sin that had us in bondage since the days of Adam and Eve. And in his Word, he says that all we must do to be saved is believe that he is the Son of God, trust him with our lives, and acknowledge that he alone is our access to eternity in heaven.

Jesus' actions prove that to God we are worth the pain, the torment, the ridicule, the bloodshed that Christ endured on that horrible crucifixion night. I've often heard it said that as Christ took in his final breath before dying, he saw the faces of all of his children — you and me and everyone who has ever lived and ever will — flash through his mind. Just to be with us, he gave everything.

But it didn't end there. The reason we can trust Christ as our perfect Sacrifice, our perfect Redeemer, is that his death on the cross wasn't the end of the story. The greatest "and then" in all of history is this: Jesus suffered and died — *and then* he rose again and went to sit in glory at the right hand of his Father!

The night I saw *The Thorn*, I realized with fresh appreciation that Christ himself — known as "a man of sorrows, and familiar with suffering" (Isaiah 53:3) — was the reason I could have hope because, ultimately, his suffering led him straight into God's eternal presence. "If anyone would come after me, he must deny himself and take up his cross and follow me," Jesus told his disciples (Matthew 16:24). Even when that cross is heavy. Even when it's excruciating to carry.

As I continued working to come to terms with my own suffering, I realized that I was indeed drawing closer to the God who created me and saved me and purposed me for a successful life (on his terms, of course). I was gaining greater proximity to the Beautifier of my ashes. I was drawing closer to the Source of all hope — to the One who promised renewed strength, eagles-wing soaring, and weariless running (see Isaiah 40:31). And whether I liked it or not, this type of intimacy with God seemed to show up only on the backside of suffering.

Coming Full Circle

The second by-product I began to experience was a healthy dose of perspective on life that had been sorely lacking when I was younger. I'd read that Romans 5 passage over and over again, each time noticing the promise that "hope does not disappoint us." In the midst of so much disappointment in my young life, I couldn't fathom that there was *anything* that wouldn't disappoint me. But there it was: *Hope* does not disappoint. And that was a perspective that I coveted.

I got a rich taste of it when I was visiting Beslan, Russia. In the aftermath of the worst school massacre in history, I met Tanya Tsarakhov. She was all of eleven years old, and with chubby cheeks, short, sandy-blonde hair, and a smile the shape of a crescent moon, she could melt your heart on first glance.

Tanya had survived the siege, but her older brother had been killed. One afternoon her mother, Olga, her younger brother, Stanislav (Stas for short), and I accompanied her to see his grave. A producer from NBC's *Today* show had made the introduction between the family and me. They wanted to portray the bond that had been formed among people half a world apart who had endured similar tragedy. The experience would solidify my belief that supernatural power, strength, and grace flow when we grieve with one another.

After we'd all piled into the car, Tanya nudged a box into my lap, a sweet grin causing her large, almond-shaped eyes to twinkle. In the midst of her overwhelming heartache and despair, she had brought *me* a gift. I was speechless — and terribly uncomfortable accepting it. But I knew I had no other respectable option. I slowly removed the box top to find a soft, pink stuffed bunny and a box of chocolate-covered cherries tucked inside. What amazing generosity from such a tenderhearted young girl!

We pulled into the cemetery, ice crunching under our tires, and soberly walked toward the grave. Olga put my hand in hers as we approached her son's gravesite. She dropped to her knees, her sobbing uncontrollable as she considered the magnitude of her loss. "Why did they kill him?" she wept. "He was just a boy! He was just beginning his life! Why did they do this?" She gripped fistfuls of dirt as she bent over the only physical remnant of her son.

I felt utterly helpless to ease her grief, but I sensed the Holy Spirit asking me to pray with Olga — with the entire family. We wrapped cold, weary arms around each other as I began talking to God on their behalf.

"Lord, please give my friends comfort and peace. Please reassure them that young Tamerlan is safe — that he's not hurting anymore. And that he is with you. God, help them to know they are not alone as they grieve, that you grieve with them and your heart breaks just as much. Please lead them and guide them, showing them where to go from here. Wrap your arms around them and speak truth into their lives. Help them all to know you more and draw closer to you during this time, and in the meantime, please draw closer to them. Soothe their pain and give them hope to carry on. This family's suffering is deep, but I ask that you would meet them where they are and walk with them, carrying them when they cannot go on. Be their light. Be their joy. Please, God, be their healing."

As we stood to our feet, we were all wiping away tears. Each of us had brought stuffed animals and candy to lay on the grave and so, one by one, we paid our respects with heavy hearts. The stuffed lamb I placed below the pole that boasted Tamerlan's precious photo began playing "Jesus Loves Me" as I slowly walked away.

I had excused myself so the family could have some time alone at the gravesite, and as I watched them from a distance as they grieved and hugged and talked, my heart swelled. In a profound moment of clarity, I felt as though I had finally accepted why Columbine had happened in my life. I was able to serve this precious family with genuine empathy for one reason only: I had walked through the valley of the shadow of death as well. And I knew the unique burden they carried as they tried to move forward from that terrible experience. Truly, my own healing was coming full circle as I found ways to help other people heal.

Sometimes, as with my experience at Columbine and the Tsarakhov family's devastation at the hands of terrorists in Beslan, suffering is caused by other people's evil and sin. Other times, we bring our suffering on ourselves, as I did when I chose to pursue popularity and ever-intensifying joyrides instead of Christlikeness. But either way, I have come to see clearly that when I am willing to walk through the pain, I gain fresh perspective on Christ's ability to overcome it. He knows me so well! He knows that sometimes the only way I will view life with his perspective is when I am struggling. Because it is then that I cry out for understanding, for answers, and for hope. And as I continue to seek purpose and comfort in the aftermath of tragedy, I can honestly say that God has heard my cries.

At one time I thought I would never heal emotionally, but of even greater concern was that I might never recover spiritually. Although I don't remember ever being angry at God, I was certainly angry at life for letting me down. And since I believed God was in control of the things that happened in life, I suppose my anger was inadvertently directed toward him. But I was too fearful to admit that. *It would be inappropriate to be mad at God. He's . . . he's God!* something inside me said.

All I knew was that I was sixteen with an entire lifetime ahead of me. And in the blink of an eye, everything was upended. I had so proudly built my house-of-cards life, but Columbine sent them all fluttering down. In the days that followed the shootings, I had become cynical: Did it really matter if I lived or died? Life is only full of disappointment and destruction and hopelessness anyway. Could death really be all that bad?

But then memories of Gam and other faithful Christ-followers would flood my mind. I knew they had devoted themselves to a higher purpose, and so I began pleading with God — would he even remember me? — to look with favor on his wayward child. *They were all right about you, but I was too blind to see it,* I remember telling him.

I realize now that Columbine gave me a gift. Columbine loosened the death grip I had on my pet sin, self-centeredness. When crouched under that table, believing beyond the shadow of a doubt that I was bound for a horrific death, I realized that the sole focus of my life to that point had been *me.* And it had left me empty, just a shell of a person trying to pretend that everything was okay.

Facing death in that way forced me to declare what I really believed — and what I really believed was that there *is* a God. There *is* a purpose for my life. There *is* hope. There *is* a Holy Spirit who will guide me into it. With Paul, I began to declare that what I had counted as profit was now a big pile of loss (see Philippians 3:7-8). Because once God fills you up, you don't crave what you craved before. The desire for popularity fades away. The money and big house and great clothes and "right" friends and "cool" hobbies fade away. They all get eclipsed by one prevailing reality: *Nothing* outside of following God matters.

When he finally had my ear, he simply whispered, "Will you stay planted in ordinary your whole life, or will you choose to be extraordinary for me?"

The Big But

A third by-product to my suffering — and what has become dearer to me, perhaps, than any other — is what Paul refers to in another of his letters to the early Christians. He tells the Corinthians that the most personally difficult challenges he had to face eventually produced an amazing result: *gratitude* for the very suffering he naturally despised.

He explains, "That is why, for Christ's sake, I delight in weaknesses, in insults, in hardships, in persecutions, in difficulties. For when I am weak, then I am strong" (2 Corinthians 12:10). In fact, God told Paul, "My grace is sufficient for you, for my power is made *perfect* in weakness" (verse 9, emphasis mine).

Perfection. Definitely not a goal we can reach as human beings. In the Old Testament God told the Israelites, "For I am the LORD who brought you up from the land of Egypt to be your God; thus you shall be holy, for I am holy" (Leviticus 11:45, NASB). But God also knew that his people could never really be like him. That's why he sent his Son and his Holy Spirit — first to make us perfect in God's eyes and then to guide us toward living out that perfection in our lives as ordinary human beings. In other words, to transform us, in spite of our weakness, into being more like him.

But how, exactly, does this happen?

What I began to realize was that God's perfecting process kicked into overdrive when I was walking through an especially painful season of trial and affliction. Seems the greater the difficulty, the more prone we are to lean into God, tucking every fiber of our being into his strong chest. In those moments, we realize with fresh appreciation our lack of control, our lack of strength, our lack of steadiness, our lack of reasonable thought. We *need* him. And we need him desperately.

In Isaiah 64:8 the Israelites are praying to God. Sure, they're known as the "remnant of God's chosen people," but they're far from perfect. In this particular prayer, they've just listed a litany of sins they've recently committed, admitting that they are unclean, unrighteous, spiritually dead, and prayerless sinners. Then, they face what I call "The Big But."

The Big But Theme occurs throughout all of Scripture and is absolutely foundational to understanding how God intervenes in our broken world. He told Noah just before torrential rains fell,

"Everything on earth will perish. *But* I will establish my covenant with you" (Genesis 6:17-18, emphasis mine). He said to Moses in the midst of issuing ten devastating plagues on the land and people of Egypt, "For by now I could have stretched out my hand and struck you and your people with a plague that would have wiped you off the earth. *But* I have raised you up for this very purpose, that I might show you my power and that my name might be proclaimed in all the earth" (Exodus 9:15-16, emphasis mine). To Job's ill-informed buddies Eliphaz, Bildad, and Zophar, he said, "I am angry with you because you didn't shoot straight with me like Job did, *but* I will accept his prayers for you and not deal with you according to the ridiculous fools that you are" (Job 42:7-8, my paraphrase). And to David and other writers throughout the fabulous book of Psalms, the examples are innumerable. Here are a few in my own words:

> I was in a slimy pit, sinking into the mud and mire, *but* God lifted me up and set my feet upon a rock. (40:2)

> I was worn out from my groaning and weeping, *but* God heard my cry for mercy and accepted my prayer. (6:6-9)

> I was walking through the valley of the shadow of death, *but* God chose to walk with me, comforting me every step of the way. (23:4)

> I was made to see troubles, many and bitter, *but* God restored my life again. (71:20)

> I was entangled by the cords of death, overcome by trouble and sorrow, *but* God showed graciousness

and righteousness and tenderness and compassion.
(116:3-6)

So back to our Israelites, who are in the middle of their prayer. They'd just acknowledged their wretchedness before God, and they summed up their thoughts this way:

> Yet, O LORD, you are our Father.
>> We are the clay, you are the potter;
>> we are all the work of your hand. (Isaiah 64:8)

This was a direct reference to God's comments a few chapters prior (not that they actually had chapters back then):

> "Woe to him who quarrels with his Maker,
>> to him who is but a potsherd among the
>> potsherds on the ground.
> Does the clay say to the potter,
>> 'What are you making?'
> Does your work say,
>> 'He has no hands'?
> Woe to him who says to his father,
>> 'What have you begotten?'
>> or to his mother,
>> 'What have you brought to birth?'

> "This is what the LORD says —
>> the Holy One of Israel, and its Maker:
> Concerning things to come,
>> do you question me about my children,
>> or give me orders about the work of my
>> hands?" (Isaiah 45:9-11)

When I saw those "woes" flying around, I realized that this was a denunciation — pretty strong language in those days. Kind of like your mom shouting your first *and* middle names when you were a kid and were in real trouble — multiplied by a factor of about one thousand.

God's anger is justified, but he still gives them The Big But:

> But Israel will be saved by the LORD
>> with an everlasting salvation;
> you will never be put to shame or disgraced,
>> to ages everlasting. (verse 17)
> But in the LORD all the descendants of Israel
>> will be found righteous and will exult. (verse 25)

When the Israelites told God in Isaiah 64 that they accepted their role as the clay and that they were willing to submit to him being the Potter, they were in essence saying, "And would you please remember The Big But from before? You know, the one where you promised that even though we are faithless and imperfect human beings, you will save us with an everlasting salvation and never put us to shame or disgrace us and somehow, someway find us righteous?"

Or, in terms I can easily relate to, "God, even though I've screwed up, would you please, please keep your promise to mold this sorry clay into something useful, something purposeful, something that can have a future and a hope?"

And miraculously, every time his children ask him to keep his promises, he keeps them. In fact, because he is the same yesterday, today, and forever (see Hebrews 13:8), he can't *not* keep them.

After each bout with suffering in my life since the devastation I experienced on April 20, 1999, I have had to face the tough question: *In my life, do I really want to be more like Christ?* Because if I do, I know that I too will have to recommit myself to being clay in the Potter's trustworthy hands. But that is one decision that is becoming easier to make because I have learned that there is an upside to suffering. It's knowing that "he who began a good work in you will carry it on to completion until the day of Christ Jesus" (Philippians 1:6).

As I continue to seek hope and purpose in the aftermath of the tragedies I've experienced and witnessed, this has become my greatest desire: to have Christ complete his perfect work in me. Regardless of how much suffering that requires.

CHAPTER FIVE

Captivated By Christ

Long ago, a Communist officer told a Christian he was
beating, "I am almighty, as you suppose your God to be.
I can kill you."
The Christian answered, "The power is all on my side. I can
love you while you torture me to death."

DC TALK, *JESUS FREAKS*

For most Americans, there is no greater evidence of our world's
brokenness than the events that unfolded on September 11, 2001. So
much has been written about the unthinkable sights, the unexpected
implications, the unmatched heroics of that day.

When 9/11 occurred, I was a sophomore at Colorado Christian
University, working through many of the same life issues that all
college students deal with: deciding what to do with my life, figuring
out the whole love and marriage thing, and undergoing changes in
family dynamics as my parents became less parent and more peer to
me. Life had finally settled down somewhat, and things were returning to normal — although normal as I had known it before Columbine
would never be seen again.

As the sun rose on that September 11 morning, I slept away. I
can't remember why now, but for some reason, I struggled to get
out of bed and was running extremely late when I punched the

radio on/off button to hear some music as I threw on my shoes. As soon as the volume kicked in, all I could hear was sheer panic on the airwaves.

I couldn't make out exactly what they were saying, so I ran into the living room that I shared with four other roommates, grabbed the remote, and flipped to the local news. Before I could get my arms around what was happening, I saw a huge jet careen into the side of the second World Trade Center tower. Although I had stood on those towers as a tourist years before, I couldn't grasp that the scene was really happening on American soil. *Surely this is a movie . . . this can't be real.*

My roommates had already left for morning classes, but suddenly, one of them walked through the front door and just stared at me with glassy eyes. We were both so confused, so afraid. We cried together and prayed together as we sat captivated in front of the TV before deciding to head to our campus chaplain's house to find out what was really going on. We wanted to know what the news reports weren't telling us. Our minds raced as we walked: *Why is this happening? Who would do such a thing? Why would God let this happen? Are we in danger here?* The whole world was starting to crumble, and all of a sudden I felt more vulnerable than ever.

An hour or so later, having already missed my morning classes, I decided to attend my third class, which was math. I had watched footage of hordes of people flooding out of the World Trade Center towers. I knew our major cities — our whole country, for that matter — were potentially under attack, and all I could think about was fearing for my life under that table at Columbine. Something had to get my mind off of what was going on. And for now, it would have to be math.

I remember feeling especially bitter toward my math teacher that morning. Despite my desire to get my mind off of things, it seemed to me that she was ridiculously distant and careless about the severity of what was going on around us. After no more than a ten-second acknowledgment of the events in New York City, she turned to the white board and said, "Well, let's get to math!"

I expected more. Needed more, even. And so I freaked.

Without necessarily meaning to cause a scene, I jumped out of my seat, drawing the attention of the twenty-five other students in the class, and began screaming at my professor, telling her that she was insane, disrespectful, and that anyone in her right mind would realize that we should all be sitting at home in front of our TVs, watching the news reports and begging God for mercy on our country and our friends in New York.

"This is a Christian school!" I demanded. "Don't we *pray* here? Don't we take stuff like this seriously? Give me a break!" And with that, I stormed out. My boyfriend, Pete Miller (who later became my husband), was in my math class, and he told me that class was cancelled after my lovely exit, the teacher obviously in shock over my outrageous demonstration.

I ran home, bolted through the front door, and glued myself to the television, determining to watch, fast, and pray for the people who had been so tragically impacted by terrorism. After an hour or so, our living room was full of my roommates and their friends, all of whom seemed oblivious to the severity of the situation. I excused myself instantly, knowing that another outburst was on the horizon and would soon be occurring if I wasn't careful. My eyes, my cheeks, and my nose were red and throbbing from crying as I holed away in my own bedroom all afternoon.

Later that evening, I could hear the living room crowd falling back into their normal routine, chatting and laughing at the usual things friends laugh at. But for me, their irreverence was a grand declaration that they had all too soon forgotten that our country was under siege. I grew more and more frustrated with my seemingly apathetic friends.

Inexplicably, the weight of the world was on my shoulders. Maybe because of Columbine, I don't know. But whatever the reason, simultaneously I felt intensely grieved by what was going on and unbelievably disappointed in my friends — in my whole "Christian" school, for that matter.

After the dust settled from 9/11, I experienced an insatiable desire to get to New York City. I desperately wanted to help clear wreckage; to pray with people who had lost loved ones; to hug the necks of scared men, women, and children who still didn't know the whereabouts of their husbands, fathers, mothers, coworkers, friends.

For weeks, I latched on to anything related to the terrorist attacks. In some small way, staying aware of the events' implications made me feel as if I were helping in some way.

Desperate to feel some spiritual ground under my feet, I found myself reading over and over a passage of Scripture that I had clung to on several occasions since the traumatic events at Columbine:

> For we know that if the earthly tent which is our house is torn down, we have a building from God, a house not made with hands, eternal in the heavens. For indeed in this house we groan, longing to be clothed with our dwelling from heaven, inasmuch as we, having put it on, will not be found naked. For indeed while we are in this tent, we groan, being burdened, because we do not want to be unclothed but to be clothed, so that what is mortal will be swallowed up by life. Now He who prepared us for this very purpose

is God, who gave to us the Spirit as a pledge.
(2 Corinthians 5:1-5, NASB)

We groan and are burdened, the text admits. My thoughts
traced back to memories of a place I'd been where the groaning
could undeniably be heard: "Kosovo" to the Western world,
"Kosova" to locals. For two Decembers in a row prior to 9/11, I
had spent two weeks in that war-ravaged region. I had seen the
fear that war struck in the eyes of entire families and the devastation it brought to their quality of life. *Were we headed for the
same plight? On American soil?* I didn't know, but I did remember what I'd learned from the people of Kosova: Despite the
suffering they had endured, their hope was not in vain. God's
guarantee of beauty and promise and a brighter tomorrow could
be trusted.

Answering a Divine Calling

Immediately after Columbine happened, Reverend Franklin Graham
had played a significant role in Littleton's search for hope and healing, even agreeing to come to our community to lead a deeply
moving memorial service in honor of the lives lost. The son of Dr.
Billy Graham and the obvious successor for presidency of the Billy
Graham Evangelistic Association, Reverend Graham was among
other noteworthy leaders such as Vice President Al Gore and
Secretary of State Colin Powell who dropped everything, it seemed,
to demonstrate their care.

Simultaneously, Reverend Graham was organizing a team to
take to Kosova in late 1999, where the war to end long-standing
disputes between Serbs and Albanians had come to an end. He
wanted the team to include students from Columbine and from
other schools that had been traumatized by violence. I think in

addition to making sure the team would feel genuine empathy for the Kosovar children who had been through so much in recent days, Reverend Graham also knew that the trip would be therapeutic for us as we reached out to others in need. He was right, of course. And Operation Christmas Child, an outreach of Samaritan's Purse, would prove to be perfectly suited to my passion for young children.

The minute I was a confirmed team member, I became Littleton's self-proclaimed poster child for Operation Christmas Child. I spoke at my church, explaining what the shoebox distribution involved and asking them to join me in filling hundreds of shoeboxes with necessity items such as toothbrushes and toothpaste and warm socks, school supplies, and toy items such as small coloring books that we ourselves would purchase. I told everyone in our neighborhood about it and even took up a collection at school. It was such an amazing time as I poured myself into an effort that would bring relief and happiness and healing to children halfway around the world. In some small way, I believed I could give back a portion of what the world had given Columbine by way of care, support, and gestures of compassion.

Prior to our departure to Kosova, I spoke at a press conference along with other team members. I remember sharing two verses from the book of Revelation that say, "They will hunger no longer, nor thirst anymore; nor will the sun beat down on them, nor any heat; for the Lamb in the center of the throne will be their shepherd, and will guide them to springs of the water of life; and God will wipe every tear from their eyes" (Revelation 7:16-17, NASB).

It's really possible, isn't it, God? I remember thinking. *Someday you really will permanently wipe away the hunger, the thirst, the pain, the suffering, the tears. You really will show us brilliant colors that we've never before seen. You'll give us perfect, angelic voices to constantly sing your praises. You'll reunite us with friends and family members whose days on this earth seemed too short. You'll make all things new.* The prospect of heaven gave me much-needed vision and energy to have a greater impact here on earth.

I would later have this confirmed in my heart while listening to a recording of a sermon entitled "Doing Missions When Dying Is Gain."[1] Originally preached by John Piper during a visit to Wheaton College, it was the most thought-provoking message I had ever heard on what it means to be a disciple of Jesus Christ. "The promise is sure, the price is suffering, but the prize is satisfaction," I wrote in my notes as I clung to Piper's every syllable.

As he explained each concept, something deep within my soul was stirred. I could barely sit still as I felt God's tender tug on my life to invest every ounce of my life in full-time ministry. I wholeheartedly believed what I was hearing: It *was* true that God's promise of maturing us in Christ was sure. And it *was* true that the prize — God's commendation of "Well done, good and faithful servant!" (Matthew 25:21) — would prove to be the one and only thing that could possibly satisfy my soul's deepest longing. But it was also true that the price for living in service to God would include suffering.

With plenty of naïveté about the amount and type of suffering it would require, then and there I decided, *That is going to be me!* The devastation of Columbine and the ensuing national spotlight catalyzed a deep desire to pour myself into something worthwhile. Now, within months of the tragedy, God was revealing what that "something" was — a heart for international missions.

Kosova was waiting. And I was ready to go.

⟡

My dad served as an adult leader on this particular trip — an added bonus, as far as I was concerned. We arrived in an exhausted state after a Dramamine-aided series of naps from Denver to Atlanta to Zurich to Macedonia. Finally in Macedonia, he and I were united with the rest of the team, and we boarded the bus for a long drive to Gjakova, Kosova.

The sights out my window reflected expansive devastation. Buildings were burned. Locals wore the chilling effects of war on their faces — faces that hadn't smiled in months. There were military reinforcements stationed every fifty yards and bomb-pitted roads that required four-wheel drive to get anywhere. Refugees from the war were living in deplorable conditions — they refrained even from walking through their own fields for fear of stray land mines detonating.

Some people are living their Columbine twenty-four hours a day, every day, I thought as I remembered that mine had lasted only seven minutes. My heart cracked with the realization that unlike my experience following Columbine, these people had no support systems, no warm beds, no cooked food, no surviving family, no shelter over their heads, no heat, no community, and no assurance that they really would have a future and a hope.

I felt certain that by God's grace, these people were going to teach me far more than I could teach them about pressing on from tragedy.

Kindred Spirits

I've always been struck by the story of Elijah in 1 Kings. Elijah had served the Lord faithfully but had come to the end of his rope. Instead of rebuking him, God showed him mercy. He fed Elijah. He gave Elijah rest. He even showed his majestic presence to Elijah through a still, small voice. But the thing that always gets me is that, in a final act of compassion, God gave Elijah a friend — a successor and an attendant named Elisha. Someone with skin who could ease life's burdens.

And that's precisely the gift God gave me in Donika.

On my first day in Kosova, our team van came to a stop in a particular village. The back doors swung open to reveal a truly captivating young woman standing on the street. She stepped up into the van, chatting immediately with the team as her long, black hair fell around her face. Her eyes were deep brown, and she had the most engaging smile. Plus, she spoke great English — an unexpected treat! She crawled over arms and legs and bags and plopped down beside me, and from that moment forward, we were attached at the hip.

Donika became my translator for our entire stay in Kosova, but more important, she became my friend. The entire team knew that we were "kindred spirits," a name I gave us, referencing *Anne of Green Gables*. Before we knew each other's stories, we shared a soul connection. The details of our life experiences would only serve to solidify our kinship and mutual respect.

Standing in Donika's backyard one afternoon, she finally filled in the blanks of her experience. Samaritan's Purse had helped her family rebuild their home after it had burned during the war. For weeks on end, Donika and her father, mother, brother, and several members of her extended family had hidden in their house from the enemy who sought to destroy them all.

They silently existed in the dark, cold, damp house with little to eat or drink. Sleep was an infrequent guest — they were all too fearful to close their eyes. Most of their energies were poured into comforting Donika's brother, Liridon, who was just an infant. Keeping him quiet was crucial to their plan to stay hidden until the war ended.

One night one of Donika's brothers was taken captive by the police, who had forced their way into the house. They threatened to burn down the house and kill him if Donika's father didn't come out of hiding. "Don't you have a mother?" Donika's mother screamed. It was as if she were pleading with them, *Have you no shame? How can you separate parent from child in this cruel, cruel manner?* Compelled by his love for his son, her dad agreed to turn himself over to the police. The boy was released to his mother, and immediately, Donika's entire family — except for her captured father — ran through the night until they reached Albania. With every step, they heard shouts and gunshots and claps of mines exploding. They were cold, hungry, and terrified.

They existed in an Albanian refugee camp for several weeks before heading back home to find the entirety of their possessions burned. Throughout the remains of their little backyard, they found blood, bullet holes, and bones strewn about.

Donika's father has not yet been found. Our conversation took place seven months after his capture, but still she held out hope for his return. "The emptiness that was created by my father's absence was filled up by God," she told me recently. "Every time I need a hug from my father, God comforts me by wrapping his arms tightly around me."

Spreading Hope

I carried Donika's story with me as our team visited other young victims of war-ravaged communities. Our mission was simple: to take vanloads of stuffed-to-the-lid shoeboxes to area children to lovingly convey that there are people who care deeply for them and that there is a God who loves them, who stands ready to deliver them peace, and who is much greater than their circumstances. For many of these kids, receiving the exact doll or toy truck they'd been praying for since they were three or four years old was just the nudge they needed to believe that this God really was looking out for them.

Our team visited a school in Kosova that had been rebuilt by a Samaritan's Purse team. It was beautiful and sunny when we arrived, and the children were lined up in nice, neat rows waiting patiently for their gifts. Never before have so many children been so well behaved!

I began distributing boxes as the lines of children came toward us and then followed them into the school to help them all open their presents. One little boy wore a smile as large as I'd ever seen. Even before he received his box, he smiled and smiled and smiled. Can you imagine after everything those little eyes had seen, he still had a smile in his heart? I thought about all the tools I had been given to process what had happened to me at Columbine — but how on earth was he supposed to understand the impact of war at his young age?

There were others who did not smile as easily. My dad had handed me a scarf to give to someone special, and during one distribution I searched and searched until I found the perfect recipient. He was sitting by himself in one of the classrooms, and as I gave him the scarf, I tried to interact with him. He was so downcast, so sad. I sat with him waiting in vain for those lips to curl into a grin. But as on so many other occasions, the traumatic experience of Columbine proved to have prepared my heart for easy, deep connection with Kosovar children, most of whom had suffered such incredible loss. I respected their need for space when they wanted it but relished the opportunity to provide hugs and laughter when they were ready.

When Donika wasn't available to interpret for me, I enjoyed the challenge of communicating nonverbally with the children. A child would find a toothbrush in his box and throw his fist up in the air, the gift tightly in his grip. I'd hold out my hand for him to place the toothbrush in my palm and then would model how to brush teeth with mock strokes, up and down, up and down. He would giggle and put his hand out to receive his gift back once more. Toy cars were good excuses to engage in tickle extravaganzas as I'd motor the little wheels over tiny arms and chubby legs and busy feet. Stuffed animals provided perfect reasons to bop expectant noses and steal gentle hugs.

Every shoebox contained a pamphlet with the gospel of Jesus in the child's native language, and many included a personalized letter from the person who prepared the gift. During one of our hospital ward distributions, a man saw us handing out shoeboxes and came by to pick up one of the gospel brochures. Several minutes later, we happened by his room to find him sitting on his bed, huddled up to the tiny window for light, reading his pamphlet. A look of peace swept over his face, and to this day, I wonder if that small seed planted ever took root in his heart. I like to believe that it did.

Welcome to the Family

During that first trip to Kosova, I had the amazing privilege of sharing my faith with Donika and her entire family. I explained that I too had been hopeless after Columbine but that Jesus was proving faithful as I learned to look to him alone for healing and stability. I slowly explained what it meant to walk with Christ — to have a friendship with the King of the universe — while Donika translated my every word to her loved ones.

The following year, on another Operation Christmas Child distribution in Kosova, I stayed with Donika in Meja, her family's village. Earlier in the year, Donika had made a trip to America. For days on end, we laughed and played and talked, visiting everything from Disney World to the mountains of my home state, Colorado. Now the tables were turned as she hosted me in her hometown.

As she and I gathered with her family in a room lit only by candles, I learned that Donika and her family had asked Christ to come into their hearts and to lead their lives. It was a moment I will never forget, because even though her earthly father never returned, they realized they have a heavenly Father who loves them and will never leave them! The family who ate every meal together, slept on mats in tiny two-room quarters together, ruthlessly supported one another, grieved lost loved ones together, and united together to rebuild their community — *that* family would now spend eternity together in the presence of the God who promised to wipe away every ounce of pain, suffering, confusion, and fear. Not to mention their buckets of tears.

Through her perseverance and newly established faith, Donika was teaching me what it meant to be a passionate follower of Christ. The unbearable pain from the wretchedness of war remained in her eyes, but my friend and her family had finally found a reason to go on.

Several months after returning home from Kosova, a letter arrived via airmail to my home in Littleton. The return address made me smile a wide smile: Donika Sokoli, it read. I opened the envelope that was bordered with red and blue diagonal stripes and found two letters, two drawings, and a simple white card inside.

As I flipped the card over, a beautiful photo of a white and purple columbine flower stared back at me. Tears chased their way down my cheeks as I sat down on my bedroom floor and began reading. Her letters were full of updates and questions and ideas for future get-togethers. Her drawings were artistically written scriptural themes she had hidden away in her heart. *You are my hiding place. You will protect me from trouble, O Lord, and surround me with songs of deliverance. Selah. Dear friends, let us love one another, for love comes from God. Be strong and take heart, all you who hope in the Lord. Now may the Lord of all peace himself give you peace at all times and in every way. The Lord be with all of you.*

I rejoiced as I considered the wonder of a new believer in Christ reading the pages of Scripture for the first time. I had given Donika a Bible before leaving her village, and her letter included a precious, carefully worded thank-you in my language:

> My Dear Crystal:
> Hello from Kosova . . . and my heart. I hope you feel strong, and that you have found happiness on your life. First of all, I would like to thank you for the Bible. In most of her page, I can find myself. And this is goin to make me moor closed with you through Jesus' words on this Bible. I pray constantly for you and your family. I miss you all so much!

Donika closed her letter with Colossians 2:8, which says, "See to it that no one takes you captive through hollow and deceptive philosophy, which depends on human tradition and the basic principles of this world rather than on Christ." She ended with,

> I am learning that I don't have to put my mind on the things of this world which are just empty and lead to nothing, but to the things what Jesus said and to practice them always.

To this day, I believe I was mercifully handpicked by God to visit Kosova so soon after my experience at Columbine. And my gratitude for the experiences I shared with families, with little children, with fellow teammates, and with my kindred spirit, Donika, will last a lifetime. Through their suffering, the people of Kosova taught me some of my earliest lessons about true healing. Through their poverty, they taught me about contentedness. Through their war-weighted smiles, they taught me about joy. And through their captivity, they taught me about being captivated by Christ.

CHAPTER SIX

Heroes of Hope

But whatever things were gain to me, those things I have
counted as loss for the sake of Christ. More than that, I
count all things to be loss in view of the surpassing value of
knowing Christ Jesus my Lord, for whom I have suffered the
loss of all things, and count them but rubbish so that I may
gain Christ, and may be found in Him, not having a righteousness
of my own derived from the Law, but that which is through
faith in Christ, the righteousness which comes from God on
the basis of faith, that I may know Him and the power of His
resurrection and the fellowship of His sufferings, being
conformed to His death; in order that I may attain to the
resurrection from the dead.

PHILIPPIANS 3:7-11, NASB

"Are you a turkey or an eagle?"

I read the question once in a book titled *Why?* by author and
speaker Anne Graham Lotz. It made me curious enough to read the
next paragraph, where she gave a little context for what my answer
might mean.

"I understand that a turkey and an eagle react differently to the
threat of a storm," Lotz continued. "A turkey reacts by running under
the barn, hoping the storm won't come near. On the other hand, an

eagle leaves the security of its nest and spreads its wings to ride the air currents of the approaching storm, knowing they will carry it higher in the sky than it could soar on its own. So, which are you — a turkey or an eagle?"[1]

There is no doubt whatsoever that we are broken people living in a broken world. The proof may be in an angry teenager with a pistol or a religious radical with a bomb strapped to her chest or a drunk sitting behind the wheel of an out-of-control car. It may be an abusive father or an unfaithful spouse or an unreasonable boss or a friend who betrays you. It may look like the death of a dream, the death of a loved one, the death of a pet. But we all have experienced suffering and trials and disappointments that forever mark us. Maybe they differ in severity or impact, but they still exist — on an ongoing and relative basis — for everyone.

Based on the particular suffering I had endured, I wondered which bird I more closely resembled. Had I run for cover, pleading with God to undo the storm, or had I spread my wings wide, confident that I would rise above the gusting winds and pounding rain?

An Eagle's Legacy

In the passage from Philippians that opens this chapter, there's an unmistakable anguish, a certain straining forward, that shows up in Paul's language. Paul's the guy in Scripture who boasted unashamedly about the dozens of trials and tribulations he'd endured.

He had worked hard and been imprisoned frequently. But he had not given up hope. Five times, he says, he received thirty-nine lashes with a whip from his abusers. But he did not give up hope. Three times he was beaten with a rod, once he was stoned by angry mobs (which typically led to death), and three times he was shipwrecked. But he did not give up hope. He had been forced to dogpaddle through the open sea for an entire twenty-four hours, he had faced near-fatal circumstances in raging rivers, and he had outrun bandits, his own countrymen, and Gentiles seeking to kill him. But he did not give up hope (see 2 Corinthians 11:24-26).

Paul sums up his suffering by saying,

> I have been . . . in danger in the city, in danger in the country, in danger at sea; and in danger from false brothers. I have labored and toiled and have often gone without sleep; I have known hunger and thirst and have often gone without food; I have been cold and naked. Besides everything else, I face daily the pressure of my concern for all the churches. Who is weak, and I do not feel weak? Who is led into sin, and I do not inwardly burn?
>
> If I must boast, I will boast of the things that show my weakness. (verses 26-30)

If anyone has an eagle's legacy, it's the apostle Paul! He was a prime example of someone who viewed the coming storms of life as opportunities to soar — to boast, even, of the fact that Christ's strength showed up in Paul's greatest times of weakness.

I should also mention, however, that he pled for mercy a time or two (well, three, to be exact). Second Corinthians 12:7-9 says this:

> To keep me from becoming conceited because of these surpassingly great revelations, there was given me a thorn in my flesh, a messenger of Satan, to torment me. Three times I pleaded with the Lord to take it away from me. But he said to me, "My grace is sufficient for you, for my power is made perfect in weakness." Therefore I will boast all the more gladly about my weaknesses, so that Christ's power may rest on me.

Nobody knows for sure what the thorn was. Was it a physical ailment or handicap? An emotional scar? An addiction or habitual sin? Could have been almost anything, according to commentators, and I actually think it's ingenious that we are left to our own imagination on this one.

Whatever it was, Paul didn't *want* his thorn. But he somehow came to grips with the fact that living with it would reveal part of God's character previously unknown to him. To him, verse 9 says, dealing with his thorn was the way Christ's power would rest on him.

The Hope Choice

As I reflected on my own journey, I could relate to Paul's struggle. Frequently, I prayed to God, *Why can't you just erase my hurt, my pain, my memories? Why won't you restore my life to how it was before Columbine, before my family broke apart, before my mind was permanently imprinted with images I wish I'd never seen? They're thorns in my flesh, God. . . . Please just take them away!*

God, of course, didn't. But as years went by, I'd find myself seeing God's face more clearly, sensing his presence more fully, feeling his hand on my life more strongly as I walked through bouts of suffering.

What was he trying to say to me? Was I really created to live a life marked by such intense disappointment?

Following Columbine, I knew that the walking, talking paradox I had become couldn't last forever. I knew I'd either find an ounce of relief from my circumstances, or I'd just curl up in the fetal position and die. *Something* had to relieve the tension of living inside the wanting-to-live-but-wishing-I-would-have-died dichotomy, but I didn't have ears to hear the "solutions" everyone offered: "Just pray, Crystal. Talk to God — he'll listen to you." "There's a purpose for all of this, Sweetheart. Just you wait. God will show you." "We don't understand God's ways, but he promises he'll cause *all* things to work together for good."

Ugh.

For the longest time, all of the clichés being thrown my way amounted to nothing more than a sickening dose of bumper-sticker theology.

As the long minutes and days and months and years ticked by, though, I developed a deep and abiding appreciation for the "useless" answers I'd dismissed before. Suddenly, it was as if my eyes had been pried open, my ears unclogged, my heart tenderized to the truth that had always been there: I had a choice to make. Hope had always been there, right by my side, waiting for me to choose it like the last kid left standing when teams are picked at recess. The choice was up to me.

Around this time I ran across a remarkable poem that shed new light on the inestimable value of suffering and its close companion, hope:

> I stood a mendicant of God
> Before His royal throne
> And begged Him for one priceless gift
> Which I could call my own.
>
> I took the gift from out His hand,
> But as I would depart
> I cried, "But Lord this is a thorn
> And it has pierced my heart."
>
> "This is a strange, a hurtful gift
> Which Thou hast given me."
> He said, "My child, I give good gifts
> And gave My best to thee."

I took it home and though at first
The cruel thorn hurt sore,
As long years passed I learned at last
To love it more and more.

I learned He never gives a thorn
Without this added grace,
He takes the thorn to pin aside
The veil which hides His face.[2]

A beggar before God asking for a priceless gift. Boy, could I relate — *Please, God, give me the priceless gift of a thorn-free life*, I'd prayed. But in truth, that's where hope had been hiding — right behind my thorns. Behind the piercing pain of disappointments, failures, travesties, and heartaches that had been wrecking my world for years. Behind them all, I realized, hope was standing by, waiting for an invitation to walk boldly into my darkness, its blazing beams of light aglow.

I could choose bitterness, or I could choose hope.
I could choose rage, or I could choose hope.
Fear or hope.
Resentment or hope.
Anger or hope.
Frustration or hope.
Chaos or hope.
Hopelessness . . .
. . . or hope.

The key was in how I responded to my thorns.

I've spent a lot of time mulling over the question, What is the essence of hope? It's a complicated thing to put words to, really. You can explain what you hope *for* and what makes you feel hope*ful*, but trying to nail down the nuts and bolts of hope itself is another story.

Hope beckons us to a bright future by constantly reminding us that there is always more. In choosing hope, a person chooses to live — chooses to pursue the truest meaning and purpose in life. Hope says yes to a person's every dream. Hope awakens the desire to go, to do, to feel, to engage when giving up seems the only logical response. Hope is the path from the desert place to the rich, lush land of abundance. Hope supplies courage to stay the course despite insurmountable odds.

There is *motion* to hope. Momentum. Forward-looking action. But there is also *stillness* — a quiet intimacy — in hope.

At times, hope is all we have to hang on to. The world can be crashing down around us in overwhelming darkness and despair, yet deep inside, a gentle voice reminds us that we are not alone. Philip Yancey observes in *Where Is God When It Hurts?* that Jesus never gave a poor or suffering person a speech about accepting his or her lot in life or swallowing without complaint the "medicine" that God had given him or her. In fact, he seemed unusually sensitive to the groans of suffering people and set about remedying them. And he used his supernatural powers to heal, never to punish.[3]

Where there is pain and suffering, we get to decide: Will we trust that we will be restored and strengthened, that there is purpose even in the pain? This kind of faith-infused hope cannot be found in ourselves or by our own strength, but in Jesus Christ alone — the hope-Giver himself, who assures us that there is beauty even in the midst of ashes. In the end, hope is simply the process of the veil being lifted — the veil that has been covering the compassionate face of God.

God had so much more planned for my life than I could have imagined. It's true: He does bring beauty from ashes. He does reveal his face when we hand him our thorns. He does deliver hope each and every time his children ask for it. He is a God who can be trusted with the entirety of our lives. It seems the clichés were true after all.

Despite how poorly I have tended to handle suffering, my deep desire is to share Paul's legacy. Once I'm long gone, I want people who were close to me to say, "Crystal? Yeah, I knew her. She was the one who was at Columbine when that shooting happened, but she didn't give up hope. She walked through some pretty tough family issues, but she didn't give up hope. There were letdowns and unexpected bends in the road and dashed dreams, but through it all, she just would not give up hope!"

It's taken me a long time to realize that I really *can* live my life this way. After all, suffering is no cakewalk. In my dark nights of the soul I've wondered if my heart would ever wake up from its numb slumber and reengage in life again. But at some point I had to *decide*, like Paul did, to fix my eyes on the prize, determining once and for all that the Enemy will not win the day. He will not succeed in suppressing my joy, my optimism, my freedom. Or my hope.

Some of the most encouraging discoveries for me have been the "eagles" in my midst. These are people who have chosen hope in the face of unspeakably tough circumstances. In fact, I've come to call them my heroes of hope. If I can glean a few life lessons from their journeys, my great aspiration is that I might then become a hope hero too.

Survived by Love

My friendship with Danny Oertli began when I was partway through my junior year of college. We were both working in conjunction with Dare2Share Ministries, a group that seeks to teach kids the importance of being bold with their faith and give them tools to do so effectively. D2S's goal is to establish thirty thousand evangelism teams nationwide and to train one million teens to clearly and confidently share the gospel by the end of 2010. When I met Danny, he was a regular musician for the tours, and I was doing promotions work for the conference circuit, connecting with youth leaders all over the nation before the event came to their respective cities.

One evening, several of us from the team were backstage following the event, and I raved to Danny about how much I loved a song of his entitled "My Last Breath." I'd never really spoken to him before, but I remember thinking how incredibly kind he was to me — especially given his status in the industry. I had the feeling he was the type of guy who would give you the shirt off his back if you needed it.

Later that year Danny was writing a song about his two children. During another backstage conversation, he shared his life story with several other team members and me, and there wasn't a dry eye in the room when he finished.

Danny met Cyndi when they were both in high school, and to hear Danny describe it, they knew instantly that they'd be together. After college, they got married, expecting a lifetime full of love and joy and companionship. But shortly after the wedding, Cyndi was diagnosed with cancer.

Danny was on the road quite a bit, pursuing his career in music, while Cyndi stayed home. She had been told that having biological children was impossible because of the chemo and radiation treatments her body had suffered through. But still she dreamed of caressing chubby feet and holding tiny hands, somehow, in some way.

Three years into their young marriage, a miracle daughter was born to Cyndi and Danny: Grace. And three years following Gracie's arrival came little Jack, by way of adoption. Danny's career was taking off — in fact, he would go on to play over a thousand different venues across the globe. Cyndi seemed to be content and health-bound. Life appeared to be smiling on the Oertlis as their dreams for a loving, nurturing family were finally coming to fruition. But their good fortune wouldn't last.

Eighteen months later, Danny was scheduled to play a gig in Hawaii. He suggested that Cyndi accompany him and that they make a vacation out of the trip — just the two of them. Cyndi had been incredibly sick and was desperately in need of some rest and relaxation. This would be a perfect getaway — a chance to regroup and reconnect after seven years filled with an unimaginable struggle to maintain health.

The days in Hawaii were a mixture of beauty and pain. Cyndi loved being away but was weary and sick the entire time. She and Danny decided that whatever was plaguing her could wait until they returned home to Denver. Upon their arrival, Cyndi's mom went with her to the doctor's office for a quick checkup while Danny stayed with Gracie and Jack, who were more than a little excited to see Mom and Dad again.

Within one hour of his wife's walking out the door, Danny received a phone call that would forever change his life. It was Cyndi's mom, calling to say that Cyndi had suffered an unexpected heart attack while in the doctor's office. Medics immediately tried to resuscitate her, but Cyndi didn't pull through.

The days and months and years that followed that event would shape who Danny was becoming as a person, a father, a follower of Christ. His journey through such heavy grief would have been unbearable if not for his caring family rallying around him day and night, loving him incredibly well.

How do you move on when you've lost the love of your life? How do you pick up the broken pieces of your picture-perfect family and try to create something worth living for? How do you walk through suffering of that magnitude without letting it suck the life right out of your soul?

In *Mommy Paints the Sky*, his book about his family's experience, Danny recounts a tender moment he shared with his kids nearly a year after Cyndi had passed away:

Grace, Jack, and I were driving down the road in my really fast Honda minivan. As we pulled into a parking space at Wal-Mart an incredible sunset began to form over the mountains. The car's interior was bathed in amber light and deep strokes of yellow criss-crossed the sky, as if drawn by an unseen hand.

"Daddy," came Gracie's little voice from the back seat, "Did God let Mommy paint the sky tonight?"

Looking in the rearview mirror I saw her leaning into Jack to catch a better view. As the light from the sunset settled on their faces, I silently praised God for the healing and hope that He had brought into our lives.

For months, I had been assuring Gracie and Jack that God had not forgotten us and that He loved us more than we could imagine. I had used big words like "sovereign" and "eternity," concepts even I didn't understand. But with the brush of His hand, God spoke to Gracie that night in a way I could not.[4]

Danny would go on to write a song by the same title in honor of Gracie's precious question. The chorus, expressing gratitude that the heavens proclaim mercy and healing in the midst of pain, ends with a thank-you to Jesus for keeping the Oertli family's hope alive through the beauty of an autumn sunset:

As if to say it won't be long
Mommy paints the sky.[5]

Danny's recognition that Jesus is the sole Keeper of hope is the reason he will forever be one of my hope heroes.

Life Rearranged

I've always believed it's in the sharing of our stories that we find the courage to live well. Somehow, sharing the good, the bad, and the ugly with each other makes our journeys manageable — it exposes the things that are common to us all: the ups, the downs, the fears, the points of celebration.

Since I was a young child, I can remember having an extraordinarily tight bond with my mom's sister, Patrice. She has always been vibrancy personified. Patrice and Mom were flanked by my two uncles, Kurt and Grant, and all four kids had lived a tough life after their family was ripped apart by alcoholism. But out of them all, Patrice was the most captivating to me.

My aunt was always confident, beautiful, and strong — but tender too. The joy she exuded was magnetizing to me as a young girl, mostly because I didn't sense the same spirit in my own mother. There was no greater compliment when I was growing up than to be told that I looked like my aunt Patrice. I would simply beam.

Aunt Patrice and her husband, Ed, have always had a magnificent relationship. These days, he is a fifty-three-year-old ultimate surfer — lives five miles from a beach in San Diego, has sun-bleached blond hair, is usually seen wearing flip-flops and long shorts, the whole bit. Ed and Patrice have fun together, plain and simple. They laugh together and cry together. They attend Bible studies together and vacation together. Most of all, there is a profound mutual respect for each other that even a casual observer picks up on.

About two years ago, I was awakened from a dead sleep by the jolting ring of my phone. "It's your aunt, Crystal," my mom said. "She has been diagnosed with multiple sclerosis."

My heart sank. More than sad, though, I was angry. *Why her? Why someone like Patrice? She's so full of life and love and energy — and now this?* My chest felt the full weight of Patrice's reality — I was so burdened for her but felt helpless to provide any support or wisdom to ease her pain.

I knew I wouldn't be able to fall back to sleep, so I got out of bed, went into the study, and read about MS for hours on end. I searched the Internet for anything I could find that would promise my aunt a fulfilling future. The titles of the various articles weren't very encouraging: "Manage MS Pain." "Dealing with Blurred Vision." "Live Well in Spite of MS." *God, please heal her. Please perform a miracle in her life that removes the signs of this disease completely — and give her life back to her.*

Evidently, Patrice had shown signs of MS on prior occasions — such as numbness in her hands and feet and limbs — but chose not to tell anyone until she knew what was causing them. When she was in her early twenties, she experienced various symptoms of the debilitating disease. Even before that, when she was only twelve or thirteen years old, Gam and Mom were shopping with her when she suddenly tumbled to the ground in a sensationless heap. She could neither walk nor talk. And although Mom's initial reaction was to giggle at her, things all too quickly shifted when she realized Patrice wasn't giggling back.

Immediately after she received word that she in fact had MS, Aunt Patrice began drug therapy via daily injections in her arms, hips, thighs, even her stomach. (I can't *imagine.*) The drugs made her so sick that she experienced massive flare-ups of her already-painful symptoms each time she took a dose. *Please, God*, I would beg daily. *Please take this disease away from my aunt!*

I talked to Patrice frequently during those first months. Despite being confused about why she had the disease, her zest for living never waned. "God is so good, Crystal. There is a purpose in this," she'd assure me. As if I were the one needing comfort. Patrice laid her life in God's hands daily, trusting him to accomplish his ways even through something as ugly as MS.

Several months after the diagnosis, I went to California to participate in an MS walk with Gam and Patrice. It was difficult to see so many "walkers" who were confined to wheelchairs. Would that be my aunt soon? Patrice was still on her feet, although each step proved more and more difficult because of the numbness and ache in her limbs.

I marveled at the throngs of people from Patrice and Ed's church who had come to the walk to support her. Her life was well lived, and even in the face of painful disease, everyone who knew Patrice knew that in her company, they would find joy. It was an amazing experience for me to witness an "eagle's legacy" playing out right before my eyes. I soaked up the lessons I was learning, desperately desiring to become more like the vibrant woman in tennis shoes and a ball cap walking slowly by my side.

The intensity of her medications made Aunt Patrice so sick that she finally went to an herbalist. Of course, insurance wouldn't cover it, but she was determined to find relief. For the past two years, Uncle Ed has had to shell out money every month for what seems like dozens of herbs and supplements — all part of Patrice's radical new diet. When she first began the plan, she almost immediately felt better. The numbness had diminished somewhat. Her weakness and sadness were subdued. Her outlook had improved. God was surely up to something, Patrice convinced herself.

But the ray of hope wouldn't last. After assimilating the new natural remedies, her symptoms returned with a vengeance. Amazingly, it seemed to make no difference to my steadfast aunt. Despite not seeing healing in her body, it was as if her soul had found rest. In the midst of agonizing pain and disablement, her faith still declared, "God can still heal me! I know God can do it!"

Throughout the entire process, God gave Aunt Patrice various images to hang on to. The most poignant is an image of stepping-stones. One night in a dream, God gave her a vision of stepping-stones along a path. Interestingly, the only stones she could make out were the large boulders immediately in front of her, just under her feet. As she peered into the distance, it seemed the path lining the way had disappeared.

Patrice determined that each stone represented a small step in her journey, and she believes the image was a signal from her heavenly Father to trust him with each one of them. In addition to big faith, my aunt possesses big talent — she can usually be caught spending her spare time in her pottery studio creating beautiful clay masterpieces or volunteering with her church's children's ministry called "Hope Street." How fitting.

Patrice's release from her suffering is her art. She sits for hours on end, soaking up the freedom that art affords her. It's a healing endeavor — mind, body, soul, spirit — and she teaches everyone around her much about trusting God to accomplish it.

I remember in the days following Columbine, Patrice and her son, Cubbie, who is not just my cousin but one of my closest friends, sent me a sympathy card to brighten my world. I still have it, and the front of it still ministers to me today. It refers to the fact that tough circumstances seem to catch us off guard and rearrange our lives, leaving us to wonder how we'll ever find the strength and courage to carry on.

Life rearranged. It's something my aunt can now relate to as well. And when my life gets rearranged again someday — which it's sure to do — my earnest desire is to reflect her optimism and strength, her passion and hope.

Great Expectations

If there's one thing Aunt Patrice taught me, it was that she had to submit her expectations for how life was supposed to be to God's will for how things are. Whether we realize it or not, our entire lives are driven by similar expectations. We have expectations for our lives, our relationships, our futures, our legacies. We even have expectations when we wake up in the morning — for how our time will be spent, who we'll see, what we'll accomplish, where we'll go. Most of the time, we aren't even aware of the expectations — until they go unmet.

Another one of my hope heroes is a woman who learned how to give God her expectations, trusting his plans to be greater than her own and trusting his outcomes to accomplish far more than her meager efforts at living well.

While I was growing up, my mom and dad had some great friends named Jim and Kris Burns. Jim was a sales rep for a wholesale plant supplier. Jim and Kris lived in Durango, Colorado, and saw my father regularly when Dad purchased stock for his landscaping business. Most summers, my entire family spent significant chunks of time at the Burnses' home. It was utopia for my dad and brother, who would walk out the back door and be inches from the Florida River, premier fishing waters for those who enjoy the sport. The property was amazing — our own slice of paradise on those hot summer days.

As I got older, Jim and Kris became more and more like family to me. In addition to being my waterskiing instructors, they taught me how to live life hospitably and energetically. Jim had children from a previous marriage who were grown and living elsewhere, so my brother and I were the sole recipients of their stellar parenting instincts. We were always adored at the Burnses' house.

On one particular afternoon, I rushed home from school — I must have been in seventh or eighth grade at the time — to show my mom a project I had done. I was so excited; I remember bounding up the stairs, shouting, "Mom! I'm home," as I ran in and out of various rooms looking for her.

I finally headed toward the master bedroom but stopped abruptly when I reached the open doorway. My mom was sitting cross-legged on her bed with photos of the Burns family covering every inch of the comforter. She barely acknowledged my presence, and instantly I knew something was horribly wrong.

Eventually looking up, her eyes stained from crying, she explained that Jim and Kris had been in an awful car accident in the middle of the night. They had been in their Suburban, driving home after having dinner with some friends in Pagosa Springs — a forty-five-minute drive. Without any warning, Jim had a massive stroke. As he lost control of the wheel, he veered onto the adjacent gradually sloped guardrail, which launched them like a guided missile into a nearby field. The huge truck flipped end over end, finally coming to a rest right side up.

Neither Jim nor Kris had been wearing a seat belt. Even now, she admits the lunacy of driving without a seat belt on, but that day — ironically — the decision may have spared them from being crushed under the weight of the truck as it tumbled through the air. Immediately upon first impact, they were ejected from the truck, along with their dog. Police reports would later confirm that Jim was thrown more than a football field's length from the Suburban, landing directly on his head.

The first person on the scene was a local automotive body shop owner. "Are you okay, ma'am? Are you hurt? Were you driving alone?" He peppered Kris with questions, but all she could say in response was, "Find my husband! Please find my husband!" When the ambulance arrived, they knew immediately that Kris was in a bad, bad state. In addition to having no feeling in either leg, she was emotionally frantic as the EMTs tried to ascertain what had happened. She kept begging them to listen, repeating, "There's someone else with me!" But the EMTs thought she was talking about her dog, and because she was frightened and in shock, they focused only on trying to calm her down.

Eventually, everyone realized that there had been another person driving the vehicle. But when they searched for Jim, they couldn't find him. When the Suburban careened across the field, it struck a transformer, knocking out all of the city's power. Masses of people scoured the area in pitch black frustration, having no idea how far from the scene Jim had landed. Reports would later reveal that he never hit the brakes — his stroke came on too fast for him to respond. The velocity that accompanied this wreck was unthinkably high. As expected, he was comatose when the paramedics finally found him.

Jim and Kris were immediately taken by Flight for Life to the trauma center at a hospital in Farmington, New Mexico. After their initial evaluation, Kris underwent a spinal cord surgery before being transferred along with Jim to Craig Hospital in Englewood, near Denver, one week later. Their diagnosis was impossibly hard for my family to hear: Kris had been categorized with a "complete injury" — paralyzed from the upper torso down and given zero chance of ever walking again. Her diaphragm was compromised. Her main organs were in shock. The mobility of her waist, hips, legs, and feet was zilch. The former all-star water-skier and consummate hostess would now be confined to a wheelchair. Forever.

During those initial days when Kris struggled with feelings of disbelief, fear, and the ugly realities of being paralyzed, her husband lay lifeless in an adjacent hospital room, his mind and body responding to absolutely nothing. Due to the force with which Jim was thrown, he was diagnosed with severe brain damage. For more than five months, Jim did not move. He did not speak. He could not swallow or breathe without full life support. His lungs had to be suctioned at least every half hour. I remember singing him songs, reading to him, and talking to him until I thought I'd fall asleep right there on his mechanically breathing chest.

Eventually, he was moved to hospice. There was so little brain activity that his condition was considered "terminal." He had opened his eyes after the first twenty days, but he had never become cognitive. After months of agonizing discussions, Kris and the rest of her family finally made the decision to remove Jim's life support. I'm sure she will never have to make a more difficult decision in her life than the one she made that day.

I had written a poem for Jim that I read at his funeral. For months on end, while Kris was working through intense physical therapy at Craig, I made journals for her and wrote her letters that highlighted various Scripture references. I never was too sure about their spiritual lives, but I wanted her to know that my love for her ran deep.

The years that followed were a tormenting season of ups and downs as Kris adjusted to a dramatically rearranged life. She was afraid. She was paralyzed. She was deflated. And even when surrounded by a roomful of people, she felt quite alone.

As I look back on the situation now, it strikes me as odd that at the time of the Burnses' accident, my own family was far from ideal in the way we lived and related to each other, yet somehow, despite our own struggles, we rallied to lend support to the Burns family. We weren't even anchored in our own faith, but strangely, God used us to serve a beloved woman in need.

Following Jim's death, Kris's doctor encouraged her to stay in the Denver area for a while. She had a strong network of friends there, and she couldn't immediately return home anyway — the house had to be remodeled to accommodate her wheelchair. She couldn't argue with their logic, so she rented an apartment in Littleton for a year.

My dad and I would often ask her to accompany us to church. One Sunday, Kris met a woman she'd heard about from her stepdaughter the previous year. Her name was Renée Bondi, a guest speaker and singer who had come to participate in worship services that weekend. Renée was also wheelchair-bound, and throughout her performance she spoke of the genuine hope she had found in Christ — hope that transformed her bleak situation into a platform on which to share the love of God all across the nation.

Kris was intrigued by Renée's spirit and expansive heart. As the two ladies grew in their friendship — spurred on by long-distance phone calls and frequent letters — Kris knew that she wanted what Renée had. She wanted her joy, her laughter, her *hope*. She wanted her optimism, her livelihood, her courage. But mostly, she wanted her peace.

And one day, she got it all when she invited Jesus to come into her heart and take control.

Kris moved back to Durango in the summer of 1997. But home wasn't really *home* anymore. Her best friend and husband was gone. Her mobility and freedom were gone. Her expectations of her "normal" daily routine were gone. Her dreams of all that life would be were gone, obliterated like the frame of that mangled Suburban.

But she had gained Christ. And though admittedly there are still "those days," Kris contends that in some strange way, it has all been worth it.

～

In sharing their stories, my intent is not to hold up any of my personal heroes of hope as saints or flawless role models. Danny, Patrice, Kris, and so many other people who inspire me are just human beings living real lives full of real situations that are far less than desirable. And they all agreed with Paul, who didn't *want* a thorn. Surely Danny pled with God to take away Cyndi's devastating cancer. Certainly my precious aunt Patrice begged God to restore her body's health. And what about Kris? She probably prayed many more than Paul's three times for God to remove her own version of the thorn and to whisper to her, "Pssst! Kris, stand up from your wheelchair and walk!"

But despite the fact that, like Paul, each of my hope heroes was stuck with a thorn, they have engaged in an unstoppable pursuit of hope — a pursuit that has revolutionized the way they look at their suffering and their lives in general. They modeled for me that once I made the choice of hope — determining that I would not be victimized by the brokenness in this world — I couldn't go back. Each time I am tempted to lie down and play dead under the weight of a new form of trauma, a tender Voice inside me whispers, "All things will be used for good — even this."

CHAPTER SEVEN

A Work in Progress

In God's presence I was;
In God's presence I am;
In God's presence I will remain.
For he is the reason I can pick up the broken pieces.
He is the reason I can stand firmly on the earth.
He is the reason I can smile and dry the tears away.
He is the reason I live, even if I die.
Through him we can learn to love again.
Through him we can be united with —
and live each day for — Jesus Christ.
Through him alone is our hope for the future.
PERSONAL JOURNAL, APRIL 2000

An artist in Colorado Springs named C. K. West created a stunning digital photographic triptych — a work of art in three pieces — called *Bitterness Removed.* As is true with powerful works of art, you can see your own life's experience right there in front of you when you stare at it. There is a plain image of a heart that appears in each of the three panels, drawing you in with its straightforward simplicity. At first glance, you might think they're all the same. But come closer. The colors and textures and lighting bravely declare that the images aren't the same at all.

The first frame features a rather gnarly heart, covered with over-lapping and tangled dead weeds. It's almost difficult to make out the shape of the heart for all of the junk it wears. If you study it long enough, you can make out the gentle red glow of the heart still beat-ing underneath it all, but honestly, all you can say about this heart is that it's constricted and enslaved.

In the second frame, all the knots and tangles and confusing veins have fallen away, and you can see the perfect heart shape emerge. The top portion is a pulsating combination of red and orange and purple and gold — vibrancy restored. The bottom portion, though, is unseen — it is hiding beneath a swath of bandages that have been gently wrapped around it.

By the third frame, the bandages are no longer necessary. The heart is full and expansive. Its luminescent, deep shades of color mirror life itself — full of motion and energy and boldness and power. You can almost make out the imperfect, nubby texture of the heart's surface, but it doesn't mind that it's flawed. It has been healed and lived to tell about everything it has endured.

Possibly my favorite aspect of the entire series, though, appears in that last frame. The straps of tangled bondage that held the heart captive in the first frame still exist. They're right there at the base of the heart, as if daring it to be healthy in spite of their presence. They didn't magically disappear or supernaturally get erased. It's just that they no longer have control.

West's *Bitterness Removed* photos brought to life a truth I have clung to on many occasions — that one reason Christ was sent to earth was to bind up the brokenhearted. He came to dress our wounds and tend to our broken hearts. Not that it was ever his design for us to exist in a fallen world, but he knew that we would. And his ministry was and still is about restoring that which is broken and undone.

My Heart, Expanded

A year after graduating from Columbine High School, I spent an entire summer in Africa serving as a Bible study leader for women and girls in a remote village of Mozambique called Canicado, just north of Maputo, Mozambique's capital. The sky at night was the blackest black I'd ever seen. Stars poked holes in the darkness, creating a living, moving Lite Brite. The moon was so brilliant that it would light your path — a perfect companion to the stars and the entire Milky Way galaxy, which stretched from end to end, glistening, active, loud.

I would awaken each morning in my little house to the joyful shouts just outside. "Mama Crissssss-tollll," young villagers' voices would sing. "Mama Crissss-tolll!" I didn't have a translator during those early morning hours, but who needed one? Love and laughter know no language.

I'd scurry about, throwing on a skirt, stuffing a piece of fresh bread in my mouth to appease my grumbling stomach, and grabbing lollipops from my secret stash (those were a huge hit among the children!) before rushing outside to play. Tiny black arms would be thrust up toward me, waiting to be spun around in circles for what seemed like hours on end. We would dance and sing and twirl and laugh until our sides hurt. I taught them how to high-five, and they believed that was about the greatest knowledge on earth a person could possess.

Most of my days were filled with playtime in the early morning, study and preparation until midafternoon, and then teaching until dinner each night. There were about thirty women and girls in my group, all impoverished and struggling to survive each day. Many had no food or clean water and existed in primitive sticks-and-straw houses. It was humbling to stand before them in the stark and dirty concrete-floor meeting hut and teach them about friendship and love and purity and trust. Who was I to advise anyone on these issues? But teach I did, although to this day, I believe I learned more than my entire group of students put together.

One afternoon as we all assembled for our Bible study, I noticed that a woman named Saineta was missing. She was a faithful attendee with a big smile — her absence was obvious. I asked the other ladies where she was, and they soberly told me through my translator that her hut had burned down. She had lost everything — not that she had much to begin with.

Instantly, our whole group rallied. Women rushed back to their own homes to pull from their meager possessions something they could give Saineta. Within minutes, it seemed, we had accumulated clothes for Saineta, her son, and the baby she would give birth to in one month's time. I had ransacked our Samaritan's Purse house and offered up what we could: plates and bowls and cups, notebooks and pens, thick wool blankets and a large mattress, baby food, and a water filter. Amazingly, my team even scrounged together ten wooden poles, straw, six pieces of metal, a door, and several nails to be used as a foundation for her new home.

I alerted part of the Samaritan's Purse ministry team who were full-time staff members working in a different village, and in no time guys showed up on their lunch breaks to start the rebuilding effort for one grateful woman. When the truck pulled up with all of Saineta's supplies, I watched as her eyes took in what was happening. Although I couldn't understand her words, her eyes said, "I can't believe all of this is for me! Why do you all care so much?"

Nobody could watch the scene unfold without getting choked up. The God of all provision was at work, making sure this sweet woman had a roof over her head and food to offer her young children that evening. Our team climbed out of the truck and grabbed stacks of goods to give to Saineta. When she registered the fact that the goods were from her local villagers, many of whom had so little to begin with, she was truly moved. What a beautiful sacrifice!

We gathered around Saineta when we were finished and offered a prayer of thanksgiving to God. Afterward, having nothing else to offer, I handed her a small wooden fish that symbolized the Christian faith. "It's not much, but maybe it will remind you who was at the center of all of this," I said with a smile. God proved once again that he could be trusted to provide. And for that, we were all grateful.

Regaining Trust

God's fingerprints were all over my life that summer in the bush region of Africa. I had seen him raise up a new house for Saineta. I'd seen hope restored for people with tuberculosis or AIDS. I'd seen women and men and children ask Jesus to come into their lives and lead them. I'd seen my own bondage broken as my habitual nightmares ceased. He had comforted me when I desperately missed my family. He had strengthened me when I thought I couldn't bear another day of challenging labor. He'd wrapped his arms of protection tightly around me night after night as I listened to the village men drinking and partying just a few kilometers from where I was staying — the place where they knew the "white girl" lived. But as I prepared to head back to the States, I realized just how little I really did trust God in my own life. Trusting him had become my crisis mode, not my default mode.

I needed to head home a week early in order to honor a speaking commitment in Idaho. Our country director and my friend Lauri had agreed to drive me to the Mozambique airport so I could fly to Johannesburg, catch a connecting flight to Atlanta, and eventually get home on time.

After waiting in line at the airport for some time, it was finally my turn. I asked the ticket agent if there would be a change fee for my flights since I was making a revision to my date of departure, but she assured me that my ticket was all I needed to get back to Colorado. With that certainty, Lauri hugged me good-bye and headed back to the city to finish her work there.

The flight to Johannesburg was uneventful. I was utterly exhausted but incredibly satisfied. I had taken away so much from my time in Africa and spent the entire flight thanking God for specific memories that I would carry with me for a lifetime.

When I arrived at the ticket counter in Johannesburg, however, my smile faded. The agent spoke with a thick accent, but I understood him well enough to catch that while it was true there was to be no change fee assessed in Mozambique, there was, in fact, a change fee to get from South Africa to the States. The cost? Two hundred and fifty dollars.

Suffice it to say, I didn't have two hundred and fifty dollars. I didn't have two dollars, for that matter. I had no cash, no traveler's checks, no credit card, no cell phone, and no hope. When the ticketing agent realized that I was nowhere near prepared to deal with the news he had delivered, he pointed me toward an adjacent customer service counter. The agent manning that desk was just as cranky as the first guy, but I tried to explain my situation with as much patience and sweetness as I could muster. Ten minutes into our discussion, with a full audience waiting in line behind me, I burst into sobs, begging him to have mercy on me.

"I'm sorry, madam, but you may not board that flight unless you pay me two hundred and fifty dollars." He was like a robot, dishing out the same response no matter how convincing my arguments became. I was trustworthy, I told him. I'd send him the money as soon as I hit American soil!

He wasn't buying it.

And I wasn't buying a ticket.

What was I going to do? I had no way out of the country. I knew no one and had no means of contacting anyone I did know.

Johannesburg — the city I was about to be tossed into alone — wasn't exactly known as the safest place on earth, especially for a young, single female from America. I prayed harder than I had ever prayed before. I prayed that the agent would realize he had made a huge mistake — that the flight didn't require a change fee after all! I prayed that some rich stranger in line would take pity on me, a poor American woman who had no way of getting home. I even prayed that I would open my wallet and mysteriously find two hundred and fifty dollars in cold, hard cash sitting there.

What I forgot to pray for, though, was that my own faith in God would increase.

I moved away from the agent's counter and stood in the middle of a wide hallway, my bags at my feet and my head in my hands. People were hustling around me en route here or there, concerned only with the clock and their gate of departure. The entire airport was spinning around me as the voices and smells and bags and lines faded to nothingness. *What am I going to do, God? What am I going to do?*

Through eyes sore from crying, I looked across several lines of people and was distracted by a man who looked like someone I had met one time. For a moment at least, this gave me something to focus on other than my distressing circumstances.

Instinctively, I shouldered one bag, picked up the other, and began walking toward him. I brushed tears away from my eyes and cheeks as my pace picked up. *Surely that's not Joe. Would I even know him if I saw him?* I had been introduced to Joe and his band members a year earlier when I was visiting my cousin Cubbie in California. But it was so long ago, and I'd only met him once. *Why would Joe be in the Johannesburg airport?*

I kept walking anyway.

"Joe!" I hollered. It seemed everyone but Joe craned his or her head toward me to see who I was talking to. "Joe? Joe!" I persisted.

Finally, his head swiveled around, and he grinned at me as recognition crept across his face.

"Hey, Crystal! What are you doing here? Are you okay?"

I dropped my bags between us and tried to compose myself so I could explain why he was absolutely the best thing that had happened to me all day. He laughed (though I didn't) as I told him how I had become stranded in South Africa. Immediately, he walked me back to the customer service counter, where he laid down two hundred and fifty dollars, cash.

Two hundred and fifty beautiful dollars. Cash.

These days, I travel differently. But I try to remember the lesson of that experience. God is worthy to be trusted with every situation in life, be it large or small, significant or trivial. He cares about his children enough to provide for them, develop them, help them, and guide them. Learning to trust again hasn't been easy — and even now, I don't have it all figured out. But this much I know: Because God has trusted me with much, I am free to trust him and to trust others.

I'm still a work in progress. But I've determined in my heart — a heart no longer as constricted by tendrils of weeds and clutter as it once was — that what God has planned for me cannot include bitterness and anger and fear and dread. Those things don't support beauty. They don't support gladness. They don't support righteousness. They certainly don't support splendor. And that is good enough reason for me.

This Devastation Is Not the End

Four years after my experiences in Africa, I would find myself in a van with five other people — one of whom was Gam, my on-location angel who had facilitated my going on the trip — riding down the bumpy remnant of a main thoroughfare in the far northwestern outskirts of the island of Sumatra.

En route, I asked our guide — I'll call him Tyler — to stop by what was left of the military base to take pictures. It — along with everything else in the vicinity, it seemed — had been leveled five months earlier by a tsunami triggered by the earth's largest earthquake in more than forty years.

At the crack of dawn on Sunday, December 26, 2004, a devastatingly powerful earthquake originated on the floor of the Indian Ocean just off the coast of northwest Sumatra. With a magnitude of 9.15,[1] it created a tsunami that roared across the ocean, claiming hundreds of thousands of lives in Indonesia, the Maldives, Sri Lanka, and Somalia.[2]

Anywhere from 275,000 to 310,000 people are thought to have died as a result of the tsunami, and the count is not yet complete. In Indonesia in particular, five hundred bodies a day were still being found in February 2005.[3] Scientists investigating the damage in Banda Aceh, the town where our team served, found evidence that the wave reached a height of eighty feet when coming ashore along large stretches of coastline, rising to one hundred feet in some areas when traveling inland. Unbelievably, the total energy released by the earthquake in the Indian Ocean has been estimated as equivalent to .8 gigatons of TNT, or about as much energy as is used in the United States in eleven days.[4]

We pulled into a small village, and I saw a man sitting in front of his lackluster store, the look on his face a combination of angst and sadness. I took pictures as we went but felt ignorant and regretful for even considering snapping one of him. *What was I thinking? He probably just lost friends or family members, and I'm treating him like a tourist attraction!*

We came to a stop and somberly made our way to a mass grave nearby. Tyler informed us that more than forty-seven thousand people were buried in that particular hole and that there were several similar graves all over the area. He'd worked on the island for more than eight years and had been on a nearby island when the earthquake set off the deadly tsunami.

Just a few weeks prior, dead bodies had lain across the median of the street where we now stood. More bodies had been packed into the river under the bridge just beside us, their eyes bulging out, their stomachs bloated from being at sea. A few hundred yards away, dump trucks had tirelessly worked slowly and steadily, pulling up to the grave and unloading hundreds more victims into the loathsome hole before covering it with dirt and rock.

Cars were overturned. Electrical and coal barges sat in the middle of the street. Children's flip-flops and tennis shoes littered the piles of rubble, each one representing a child who would never have the chance to grow up.

There were no words, no thoughts, no feelings that could come close to capturing the devastation. We bowed our heads and prayed for the families of those people who were buried there, trusting God to somehow fill the enormous void they all felt. I opened my eyes as Tyler finished praying and saw two butterflies fluttering around us, hopping from peak to peak of the rubble.

Life prevailing over death, all in one frame. It was the miniscule ounce of uplift I needed.

As we walked back to the car, I noticed that Tyler had run up ahead and was talking to the man I'd seen previously. As I got closer, I saw that the man was sobbing, pulling himself together every few seconds to sop up his tears with his shirt. Tyler had given the man a uniform for his son, a coloring book, and two bottles of vitamins. He sat down beside the grief-stricken man and put his hand on his back to comfort him. With Tyler interpreting every word for our team, Santoso tearfully shared his story.

"I was at my store by the water's edge when I saw big waves on the coast. I jumped onto my moped and drove through the town warning people that the water was coming. Some people believed me and ran, but others didn't believe at all. I went quickly to my house to get my wife and my two boys, but as I neared the house, I saw the main wall collapse onto my wife and my oldest son. He was only fourteen years of age.

"My youngest son — who is ten years of age — climbed onto a pillar. It was the only one left standing, and he held on for his life. I climbed up a tree and held on as well. The waters came. My family — there were more than twenty of us — were all taken by the water. Just my young son and me, that is all that remains."

As it turned out, the vast majority of people who lived in the three villages that Santoso had been able to warn had survived. The one he didn't get to suffered a loss of more than ninety percent of its residents.

We cried with him and asked how we could serve him.

"I am touched that you will stop and listen and cry with me," he said through his tears.

I stepped back and focused intently on Santoso's eyes. They silently pled for relief from the pain. It was as if I could hear him say, *Help me. I can hardly breathe. My heart is so heavy and overwhelmed with sadness. So many stories. So much loss. So much devastation. Who will sit with me and listen? Who will cry with me today? Broken and alone I rest, with only my memories to cling to. Just feet away, the mighty ocean gently rolls — the same waters that took my family away forever. Come to me, please, and I promise to hear the truth. Finally, my heart is open. Now tell me, is there any hope?*

It struck me that literally tens of thousands of people representing hundreds of relief and emergency care organizations had come through this village but had never stopped to listen. There are millions of stories to be told in Indonesia but so few ears to hear them. What an impact we could make for God's kingdom if we would not only rebuild houses but also put our efforts into rebuilding lives!

I looked behind the place where Santoso was sitting and noticed his new store. He had to stay in business somehow in order to support his son, but the shack I saw before me seemed a paltry means to a living. Its floor consisted of thousands of brick shards strewn everywhere, and his wares on display included only three small cans of soda, two bottles of water, and a few insignificant items.

We asked if we could pray for him and, amazingly, he agreed. All of us wept throughout the entire prayer. When we finished, I looked directly into his eyes and promised him that this devastation would not be the end. I knew I would never forget Santoso — I'd never forget the look on his face as our team listened intently to his story.

When we had driven up to the remains of that military base, I had merely wanted to take a picture. Instead, God showed me one — a picture of one beautiful life spared in the midst of unthinkable loss. It's one I can't develop and frame, but it will live in my mind and heart forever.

Strength for Today, Hope for Tomorrow

One afternoon, our team drove to a small tent city — a town that once had nearly thirteen thousand villagers, only two thousand of which remain today. The morning of the tsunami, the town's entire leadership group was on the beach holding a meeting. The wave hit, killing every single one of them. The village was left with no one in charge, so they appointed Wahyu, who now leads those who survived.

Wahyu had seen the water coming and had tried to run toward the hills. He took his mother with him but was ultimately unable to save her from the angry sea. For one week's time, according to Wahyu, not one person came to his family's aid. He survived on coconut milk and rotted fish that had washed on shore. He wore the same sarong day after day — his only remaining garment — and told us how very cold he was at night when the temperature dropped.

We stepped over stumps and concrete foundations on our way to an area that had been badly hit. As I took each step, I realized I was walking in the middle of what used to be people's living rooms and kitchens and bedrooms. The ocean had swept everything away. We finally arrived in front of one of the barges that had washed in with the wave. It hit me as I stared up at the three-hundred-foot-long structure just how fierce the water must have been. It had carried the barge over houses and trees and plunged it down on the village's rooftops while terrified people remained inside.

I went back to our house that night and cried until my eyes burned. The sights of the day were intense and jarring. I knew that God was sovereign even in the midst of the devastation I'd seen, but everything seemed so out of control. So unpredictable. So shaky and fragile and tenuous. I wrote for hours in my journal while I listened to my Tim Hughes CD over and over and over again. His song entitled "Whole World in His Hands" — a simple, honest explanation of what it means to really trust God — gave me some relief from the agonizing grief I felt.

During most days, our team set up medical clinics for people in the community to receive checkups and be checked for disease by American doctors. While their parents were being examined, I played with the children. We jumped rope, colored together, took pictures, and played with toys. Every adult I met had lost at least one family member — and some had lost up to twenty-one. They were merely surviving, existing with a strange vacancy in their eyes. They had no food, no clothing, and no peace. They served a god who they believed had exacted his wrath on his people through this horrifying event. "We repent, Allah," appeared in their language on the sides of any remaining structure that would take spray paint.

We did whatever we could to show these people authentic love. We asked children to show us with crayons and paper what the experience had been like, and we were astounded by the results. It was therapeutic for those kids to express what they had been keeping inside for five months' time. Some drew pictures of the wave itself; others drew people clinging to trees or poles; others drew helicopters in the sky attempting rescue operations; still others drew cars overturned or trees upside down.

For his crayon drawing, one young boy even depicted a bright, colorful rainbow that covered the entire sky — proof that things would one day get better. I doubt he knew the biblical significance of that image, but I smiled at his faith nonetheless.

The next morning, we went to set up for a clinic at a local mosque. Such structures were some of the only ones that had survived the devastation. The floors looked like milky white marble and still seemed proud of their beauty despite the fact that the walls surrounding them bore gaping holes created when the waters had swept through. When we looked through those holes toward the nearby community, we could see tents that people now called home and new bodies of water that had formed after the storm. On one side of the building, there was a large curtain that could be drawn to cordon off the main room — customary accommodation to allow men to pray while women and children are present. As a gesture of respect, we took off our shoes upon entering the building that these villagers viewed as utterly sacred.

The clinic that day was slow at first, just a handful of villagers in line for checkups. But soon the place was packed with families, the parents curiously watching us color with their kids while they waited for their exams. The floor beneath their feet pulsated with dozens of tiny, wriggling bodies, all stomach-side down as they created their crayon masterpieces. Eventually, as giggles flooded the room, parents gave in and joined us in our coloring escapade on the cold, hard floor. It was small relief for these men and women who had been through so much. But it was therapeutic all the same.

Throughout my time in Indonesia, people constantly asked me whether I was Muslim or Christian. Out of deference to their culture, I faithfully wore a jilbob, which is what the locals called my shoulder-length head covering. My response to their question was always the same, always delivered with a smile: "Pungikoot Isa Almasy" — *I am a follower of Jesus the Messiah.*

This answer carried with it several connotations, since it was obvious that I am American and therefore a Christian in their estimation. Muslims in that part of the world believe that the entire Western world is Christian and that Christianity is just a wild combination of *Baywatch*, MTV, and *Desperate Housewives.* I desperately wanted to distinguish my faith from this errant perception.

Islamic traditions and practices were pervasive on the island. Five times daily, activity ceased as prayers to Allah were offered over the loudspeakers positioned all around town. How I admired their devotion and commitment. I dreamed about what would happen if Christ-followers became that devoted to their faith in God. Just imagine the impact!

Someone once said that hope is desire accompanied by expectation. That was an image I could relate to as I saw the devastation in Indonesia. I desperately wanted relief for those people. And I truly believed that one day, many of them would find it.

Overcoming Aftershocks

Obviously, the effects of the tsunami still reverberate. Just after three o'clock one morning while our team was there, our entire household awakened to a trembling world. I was terrified as I jumped out of my bottom bunk bed, afraid that the top bunk would come crashing down on my head. Five other girls were in the room, and nobody knew what we should do. Should we leave the house or stay put? Would anyone even hear us if we screamed?

I learned all too quickly that aftershocks were commonplace on the island. At least twice weekly in the months that followed the tsunami, aftershocks measuring 5.2 or higher rumbled through the town, shaking the stability of villagers and catalyzing evacuations of entire towns that feared the waters would come crashing in again. The ongoing horror these people were enduring was almost beyond imagination.

Like so many others around the world, the people of Indonesia are still living with appalling effects of their suffering. They live in tents on slab foundations. They eat "relief food" — prepackaged pouches of instant soup or rice or cornmeal. They mourn their lost loved ones. And all the while, the rest of the world moves on.

The issue is this: We *can't* just move on, because each one of us has aftershocks from our own bouts with suffering, whether large or small. And if each of us is actively concerned about the rest of us finding hope in the midst of earth-shattering losses, we will all be healthier. The challenge for anyone straining to live in hope's reality is to fend off cynicism. It's a battle, in and of itself, to believe — really believe — that our individual efforts can make a difference. But I suggest that we try. The best way to witness tangible proof of God's ever-present hope is to accept the challenge to help, to serve, to love, to heal. As followers of Christ, this is not only our responsibility; it is our privilege.

The most important thing we can do is determine *now* how we will respond when suffering hits. Who will we follow? Will we follow Christ, the One who has promised to unveil hope in the most unlikely of places — just behind our suffering? Or will we follow our own ideas and whims and prejudices?

I've chosen to invest myself in serving the world around me. And based on what I've seen, I assure you that there is a world in need, waiting for you to be the banner carrier of hope for such a time as this. Find your Kosova, your Beslan, your Indonesia, and go! Maybe it's your own family that could use a little hope. Or maybe it's someone halfway around the world. The distance isn't the issue; your heart's posture is.

I don't know where you've been, what battles you're currently fighting, or what suffering awaits you in the days and months and years ahead. Regardless, my encouragement to you is to press on, humble clay, knowing that your Potter loves you with an everlasting love. As I promised the tenderhearted Indonesian man, Santoso, on that cloudy day several months ago, this devastation — whatever yours might be — is not the end.

How do I know, you ask? Because *Pungikoot Isa Almasy*. I am a follower of Jesus the Messiah, Son of the living God, who has the whole world in his hands.

Living It Out

Without your wounds where would you be? The very angels themselves cannot persuade the wretched and blundering children of earth as can one human being broken in the wheels of living. In love's service, only the wounded soldiers can serve.

THORNTON WILDER,
"THE ANGEL THAT TROUBLED THE WATER"

God is going to get me out of here alive, and I will have an incredible story to share. I remember having this thought as I wrestled with reality under the library table that awful day at school. The idea was absurd to me even at the time. I mean, it was obvious that I was about to be killed. But something inside of me wouldn't let go of the nagging, reverberating belief that said, *I will get out. I will have a story to share. God will deliver me from this nightmare. In spite of this event, he will still somehow get glory.*

The prayer for salvation I'd prayed years before with Gam was a sincere one, but I remember recognizing that this was the first time I had truly pursued God. Some people might say it was only a foxhole confession, but everything in my mind, spirit, body, and soul really did desire to live a new life. I desperately wanted to begin living beyond myself, never to look back again.

In the months ahead, despite the chaos surrounding me, despite the still-nagging questions about why some students survived and others didn't, despite even my waning commitment to God in the first place, I had an overwhelming sense of God's purpose in the whole ordeal. It was as if a single promise in the Bible had finally burst through my resistant heart. God says to us all, "[I] will never leave you nor forsake you" (Deuteronomy 31:8). I knew that God was going to use the event — in all of its horror — to bring glory to himself. I now see that this was just the beginning of a beauty-from-ashes trend that would eventually play out all over my life. To this day, I believe that everything I endured at Columbine would be in vain if I neglected to fulfill the amazing purpose God has wired me for.

Columbine and its many implications in my young life were devastating, no question about it. But it was underneath that four-foot table that I received my initial "calling" into ministry. I don't know if the experience was the *only* way God could have gotten my attention. But I do know that what I hoped for as bullets rained down around me came true: The story God had given me to tell could indeed radically change the lives of people who heard it.

Rachel's Challenge

A few weeks after Rachel Joy Scott's tragic death in the grassy area outside our school, her family was going through her belongings and found an assignment Rachel had written for class just a month before she was killed. It was called "My Ethics, My Codes of Life."

It was a class project that she had used as an opportunity to share what she believed. The content of that project exemplified all that it meant to be Rachel Scott. She wrote, "I have this theory that if one person can go out of their way to show compassion, then it will start a chain reaction of the same. People will never know how far a little kindness can go." Rachel knew that things like compassion and kindness would indeed go a long way toward "making the world a better place and making each person's life a better one to live."[1]

Rachel had already taken up her own challenge, determining to reach out to those who were mentally, physically, or otherwise handicapped, those who were new to the school, and those who were picked on. Despite the ridicule she received from friends in her circle, she persisted in living out her mission. As a result, she dramatically influenced dozens of lives.

During my own high school days, I didn't know Rachel well at all. Frankly, I was too concerned with being popular to hang out with her and her friends, most of whom were considered less than cool by my crowd. But although I ran with a different group of people, secretly I deeply respected Rachel Scott.

I grieve the fact that I was "too good" for Rachel while she was alive. What's uncanny is that I missed out on her friendship for one stupid reason alone: While she was diligently being all God intended her to be, I was too busy trying to be someone I was not. It's a reality I will forever regret.

So much had shifted in my heart by the time I went to Colorado Christian University. Speaking to large crowds was fast becoming my most prominent act of worship. A talk was never just a talk; instead, it was a powerful way to say thank you to the God who himself spoke the world into existence, the God who has given me a unique story to tell, and the God who wired every single audience member with a purpose that will bring him glory if it is seized. I loved being the carrier of his hope-message and seeing light bulbs flicker on in people's minds.

One day during my sophomore year at school, I remembered hearing that Darrell Scott, Rachel's dad, was organizing speakers to work with the Scotts' organization, Rachel's Challenge. Their goal was simple: to inspire, instruct, and enable students all over the world to bring positive change to their school environments.

Through use of powerful video and audio footage of Rachel's life and the Columbine tragedy, they motivate kids to treat others with respect, dignity, and love. Untold numbers of people — including celebrities in Hollywood, in government, on the sports field, and in academia — have been heavily influenced by Rachel's Challenge. Even two presidents of the United States have rallied around this effort. Students are the target audience, and they have proven that they will respond with positive words, attitudes, and actions.

Rachel's Challenge carries a message of nonviolence. A message of hope. And it was a message I desperately wanted to help spread. I contacted Darrell Scott's agent and asked how I would go about joining the team of speakers. For starters, Darrell suggested that I watch a presentation live to see if my style would gel with the spirit of Rachel's Challenge. The next one would be in Highlands Ranch near Denver.

After sitting through the moving, hour-long presentation, I found myself utterly stunned. Tears had streamed down my face for the vast majority of the talk, and God was gripping my heart in a profound way. "One person can step out and start a chain reaction!" Darrell had said during his closing. "But just imagine what would happen if an entire school took up the challenge today — the challenge to stand up against mockery and bullying and anger and exclusion. Don't leave here unchanged. Reach out to the new kids in your school, the physically and mentally handicapped, and those who are picked on. You never know when your single act of kindness just might start a chain reaction."

How I wished I were a high school kid again so that I myself could accept the challenge!

Redeeming What Was Lost

I could never go back to my high school days. I could never retrieve the opportunity to walk through life with Rachel as my friend. I couldn't wave a magic wand and undo the hurtful attitude I'd had or the aloofness in my spirit toward Rachel and her friends. I still can't.

But there was something I could do. I got in touch with Darrell once more, and he consented to having me deliver a couple of talks at schools they'd just booked in York, Pennsylvania. As I spoke to the students at that first venue about the power of starting a chain reaction of kindness and compassion in their world, I knew deep inside that there would be something very redeeming about linking arms with other speakers and leaders who desired to see Rachel's legacy change lives. In one role or another, I have been part of the Rachel's Challenge team ever since.

Rachel's story has touched so many people, many of whom are incredibly influential in the world. These days, Darrell's full-time job is centered on sharpening Rachel's Challenge to make it more powerful and more pervasive. His goal? That every single student in America would have the opportunity to start a chain reaction of kindness and compassion in their world — that they would live out the reality that each person can make a difference for good in this generation.

As of 2004, based on firsthand information Darrell has received from community leaders and school personnel, seven known school shootings had been prevented or stopped because of Rachel's Challenge. All because at least one student made the simple decision to hold a door open, offer a smile, sit with someone at lunch who was alone, or manifest a heart of compassion in any of a thousand other ways. From there, the ripple just rolled.

My prayer is that everyone who reads this book will seize the opportunity to take Rachel up on her challenge. Decide now what you stand for and make sure the people closest to you understand why. Decide now what your legacy will be — after all, tomorrow is not promised to any of us. Decide now that even if people intend you harm, you will trust God to bring beauty from ashes. And then act! Take the first step toward compassion. Toward love. Toward freedom. Toward faith. In doing so, you just might spread kindness in a world that is cruel. You just might spread joy in a world soured by sin. You just might be a light to a world full of darkness. And in starting your own chain reaction, you just might be the one who can hold out the priceless gift of hope.

Notes

Introduction: Giving It All Away
1. "New Video of Beslan School Terror," *CBS News*, January 21, 2005, http://www.cbsnews.com/stories/2005/01/20/48hours/main668127.shtml.
2. "New Video of Beslan School Terror."

Chapter 1: Columbines Everywhere
1. "A Time Line of Recent Worldwide School Shootings," *infoplease*, 2005, http://www.infoplease.com/ipa/A0777958.html.
2. "A Time Line of Recent Worldwide School Shootings."

Chapter 3: Three Steps Forward, Two Steps Back
1. Anne Lamott, *Traveling Mercies: Some Thoughts on Faith* (New York: Anchor Books, 1999), 195.
2. Donald Miller, *Searching for God Knows What* (Nashville: Nelson, 2004), 113.

Chapter 4: The Upside of Suffering
1. Howard Hendricks, "How to Be Spiritual Without Being Phony" (men's retreat, session 2, Woodmen Valley Chapel, Colorado Springs, CO, April 2, 2005).
2. Robert Lowry, "Nothing but the Blood of Jesus" (New York: Biglow & Main, 1876).

Chapter 5: Captivated By Christ
1. John Piper, "Doing Missions When Dying Is Gain," audiotape of sermon presented at Wheaton College, Wheaton, Illinois, 1997, for Desiring God Ministries.

Chapter 6: Heroes of Hope
1. Anne Graham Lotz, *Why? Trusting God When You Don't Understand* (Nashville: W Publishing, 2004), 25.

2. "The Thorn," attributed to Martha Snell Nicholson at http://www.desiringgod.org/library/sermons/01/051301.html.
3. Philip Yancey, *Where Is God When It Hurts?* (Grand Rapids, MI: Zondervan, 1990), 82.
4. Danny Oertli, *Mommy Paints the Sky* (Colorado Springs, CO: NavPress, 2004), 137–138.
5. Oertli, 139.

Chapter 7: A Work in Progress

1. "2004 Indian Ocean Earthquake," *Wikipedia*, http://en.wikipedia.org/wiki/2004_Indian_Ocean_earthquake.
2. Helen Lambourne, "Tsunami: Anatomy of a Disaster," *BBC News World Edition*, http://news.bbc.co.uk/2/hi/science/nature/4381395.stm.
3. "2004 Indian Ocean Earthquake."
4. "2004 Indian Ocean Earthquake."

Epilogue: Living It Out

1. Excerpted from Rachel's Challenge brochure.

About the Author

Crystal Woodman Miller is a full-time speaker who has delivered her message of hope to tens of thousands of people both domestically and internationally. Having ministered in places such as El Salvador, Honduras, Russia, Mozambique, Belize, and Kosova, Crystal also speaks regularly at high schools, churches, rallies, community events, and memorial services across the U.S. She has appeared on the *Today* show, *Good Morning America*, and the Billy Graham Evangelistic Association's 2005 national broadcast, which aired a five-minute segment profiling Crystal. In addition to her personal speaking ministry, Crystal currently serves as an assembly speaker with Rachel's Challenge; an associate evangelist with Dare2Share Ministries; and a national spokesperson for Operation Christmas Child, a project of Samaritan's Purse.

Crystal is a 2004 graduate of Barclay College, where she earned a bachelor's of science degree in Christian leadership. A former resident of Colorado, she now resides in Edmond, Oklahoma, with her husband, Pete Miller. For more information on Crystal's ministry or to contact her regarding speaking opportunities, visit www.crystalmiller.org.

LEARN TO GET REAL WITH GOD AND YOURSELF.

Honest to God
Charlie W. Starr
1-57683-647-9

Examine some of the most important and honest characters in the Bible—Abraham, Jacob, David, Jesus, and others—and learn what they knew about God. Find out why wrestling with the truth can actually bring you closer to Him.

Redefining Life: My Purpose
1-57683-827-7

In this discussion guide you will be challenged to ask yourself some tough questions about your significance and where you find it.

Redefining Life: My Identity
1-57683-828-5

There is freedom in knowing who you are, and this discussion guide will help with the process. You'll not only discover what you were created for but also learn about the One who created you.

THINK

NAVPRESS
BRINGING TRUTH TO LIFE
www.navpress.com

To order copies, visit your local Christian bookstore,
call NavPress at 1-800-366-7788, or log on to www.navpress.com.
To locate a Christian bookstore near you,
call 1-800-991-7747.